WHAT GANDHI SAYS

WHAT GANDHI SAYS

About Nonviolence, Resistance and Courage

NORMAN G. FINKELSTEIN

O/R

OR Books

New York • London

© 2012 Norman G. Finkelstein

Published by OR Books, New York and London.

OR Books is a new type of publishing company that embraces
progressive change in politics, culture and the business of
publishing. We sell our books worldwide, direct to readers.
To avoid the waste of unsold copies, we produce our books
only when they are wanted, either through print-on-demand
or as platform-agnostic e-books. Our approach jettisons the
inefficiencies of conventional publishing to better serve readers,
writers and the environment. If you would like to find out more
about OR Books please visit our website at **www.orbooks.com**.

First printing 2012.

Cataloging-in-Publication data is available from the Library of
    Congress
A catalog record for this book is available from the British Library

ISBN 978-1-935928-79-9 paperback
ISBN 978-1-935928-80-5 e-book

The typeface in which this book is set is Amalia. Typeset by
Wordstop Technologies, Chennai, India.

To the "Occupy" movement

TABLE OF CONTENTS

ACKNOWLEDGMENTS

I am grateful for the Unz Foundation's support, and for the comments on earlier drafts from Samir Chopra, Antony Copley, Meghna Kumar, Sanjeev Mahajan, Karuna Mantena, Allan Nairn, Abid Qureshi, Marco Rosaire Rossi, Feroze Sidhwa and Doug Tarnopol. As always, my biggest debt is to my editor, Maren Hackmann-Mahajan.

INTRODUCTION

Although Mahatma Gandhi's name is frequently invoked, he is seldom read.

While checking out his collected works from the library of a solid American research university, I noticed that of the nearly 100 volumes in the Gandhi corpus, each of which runs to some 500 pages, only one volume had previously been borrowed.

Gandhi has been reduced to a mantra equating his name with nonviolence.

But his thought and practice are much more complex, and contradictory, than this formula suggests.

The Gandhi bequeathed by history is a watered-down, saccharine version of the original. He is the saintly, other-worldly eccentric who would not hurt a fly, and looked as if he could not even if he were so inclined.

The real Gandhi was indeed saintly, otherworldly and eccentric, but he was also the shrewdest of political tacticians who could gauge better than any of his contemporaries the reserves and limits of his people and of his adversaries.

The real Gandhi did loathe violence but he loathed cowardice more than violence. If his constituents could not find the inner wherewithal to resist nonviolently, then he exhorted them to find the courage to hit back those who assaulted or demeaned them.

If Gandhi preached simultaneously the virtues of nonviolence and courage, it was because he believed that nonviolence required more courage than violence.

The violent combatant faced enemy gunfire with weapon in hand, whereas the nonviolent resister was expected to march headlong into enemy fire "smilingly" and "cheerfully" as he was blown to bits.

Those who used nonviolence not to resist but instead as a pretext to flee an assailant were, according to Gandhi, the most contemptible of human creatures, undeserving of life.

The controversial Gandhi who valued courage above nonviolence, who valued nonviolence because it required the maximum reserves of courage, and who advocated violence if one could not muster this courage, has been largely forgotten, or effaced.

But even the Gandhi who is remembered perplexes.

The doctrine of *satyagraha* that Gandhi propagated was deceptively simple.

It denoted nonviolent resistance to evil, didn't it?

But Gandhi equated violence with any form of coercive force.

Still, he counseled the impoverished Indian workers and peasants to mobilize their latent *power* in order to break the will of the exploiting classes.

It was also never quite clear whom Gandhi was trying to reach with his nonviolent resistance.

Sometimes he spoke about wanting to melt even Hitler's heart.

But at other times Gandhi directed his fasts at the broadly sympathetic public. He undertook to "quicken" its conscience and get it to act on what it already knew was wrong in order to isolate the handful of diehards.

∞∞

This little book attempts to distill the essence of Gandhi's doctrine of nonviolent resistance.

Although Gandhi's preachments are replete with blatant contradictions, and are informed by a religious faith not always amenable to rational analysis, it is still possible to tease out a coherent doctrine from the record he left behind.

But mine is not just, or even primarily, an academic exercise.

Bringing to bear a keen mind on a rich life experience of public service, Gandhi extracted valuable practical insights into the nature of politics, which it would be imprudent to ignore.

I first began to read Gandhi a few years ago in order to think through a nonviolent strategy for ending the Israeli occupation of Palestinian lands.

But the field for the application of Gandhi's ideas has now been vastly expanded by the emergence of the Arab Spring and nonviolent resistance movements around the world.

Gandhi's name is everywhere on the lips of those challenging a political system that shuts out the overwhelming majority of people and an economic system that leaves them futureless.

In my own city of New York, the idea of nonviolent civil disobedience has seized the imagination of young people and energized them with the hope that they can bring even the ramparts of Wall Street tumbling down.

Gandhi devoted the whole of his adult life to organizing the powerless 99 percent against the greedy 1 percent. He aspired in the first place to end the British occupation of India, but he also recoiled at the prospect of a corrupt clique of native Indians replacing the foreign occupiers.

Gandhi sought to lay the foundations for a political system in which not just nominal but also actual power was transferred to the Indian masses, and in which wealth was equitably distributed but the chase after wealth ceased to be life's purpose.

He was convinced not only that the old world could be extirpated and a new world be brought into being nonviolently, but also that unless it was done nonviolently, the new world would hardly differ from the old world it superseded.

A new generation is now experimenting with and envisioning novel ways of living, and pondering how to redistribute power and eliminate privilege. The life experience and reflections of Gandhi provide a rich trove to help guide these idealistic but disciplined, courageous but cautious, youth as they venture forth to create a brighter future.

1/ INNER VOICE

It is not easy to present a comprehensive or coherent picture of Gandhi's doctrine of nonviolent resistance or *satyagraha*.[1]

As noted in the introduction, Gandhi's collected works come to some 100 hefty volumes. I have read about half this corpus,[2] as well as several anthologies,[3] biographies and scholarly studies. My remarks will therefore be partial in a single and perhaps double sense. They will not encompass the full breadth of Gandhi's reflections. My reading focused on the period 1930–1947, when Gandhi's doctrine was put to its severest tests. But this was also the period when his thinking had fully ripened.

Because of my incomplete reading, I arguably missed crucial transitions and ruptures in Gandhi's thought, and consequently I will have presented a snapshot of a mind at work rather than the moving picture. But, although he lived a long, rich life, and one relentlessly subjected to self-scrutiny, Gandhi stayed steadfast in his bedrock beliefs. "Whenever I have been obliged to compare my writing even of fifty years ago with the latest," he observed, "I have discovered no inconsistency between the two."[4]

Gandhi acknowledged local errors[5] and reversals of judgment,[6] but there were no "God that Failed" recantations or "Second Thoughts" epiphanies. His one systematic philosophical exposition is a slim, seemingly idiosyncratic volume titled *Hind Swaraj* (Indian Home Rule) that he quickly penned in 1909.[7] Reflecting on this book at various junctures much later in his life, Gandhi expressed full satisfaction with it.[8]

Still, Gandhi's life and writings were shot through with contradictions. He liked to quote Ralph Waldo Emerson, "Foolish consistency is the hobgoblin of little minds."[9] It is a misfortune of the little minds trying to make sense of him that Gandhi was a consistent exponent of this quip, as he attached little value to consistency: "Charges of . . . inconsistency ought not to matter. What must count with a public servant is the approbation of his own conscience." But Gandhi would also insist that he himself was consistently consistent: "Inconsistency is only apparent. It appears so to many friends because of my responsiveness to varying circumstances. Seeming consistency may really be sheer obstinacy."[10]

The fact is, Gandhi's actions often did belie his words. In his defense Gandhi argued that inconsistency was unavoidable in the application of a theory: "my nonviolence cannot deviate from what is practical"; "no one is able to act upon a great principle, like that of nonviolence, in its entirety"; "pure unmixed nonviolence is as impossible as Euclid's line."[11]

At the inception of his political career Gandhi recruited an ambulance corps for the British side in the Boer and Zulu wars.[12] He again offered during World War I to mobilize an ambulance corps for the British army, and then recruited Indians to take up arms and fight alongside Britain.[13]

The world's most famous exponent of nonviolence later even sanctioned "calling in the army and having a handful of men shot" to stop inter-communal rioting among Indians.[14] Gandhi also acquiesced in India's military cooperation with the Allied war effort during World War II if the British granted it independence, and the deployment of Indian troops after partition to prevent Kashmir's secession.[15]

Throughout his life Gandhi would insist that his active wartime partisanship early in his political life did not contradict his doctrine of nonviolence.[16] But on this point (and many others) his reasoning did not carry conviction.[17] Although trained as a barrister, Gandhi was not a persuasive dialectician. When interrogated by a shrewd critic, he seldom had a compelling repartee and more often than not lapsed into mumbo-jumbo. "I do not think that on the whole your argument is coherent," one of his early critics fairly observed, "or that the various statements and opinions you express have any real dependence upon one another."[18]

But Gandhi did not just fail to acknowledge the gap between his actions and words. He also resorted to the ex cathedra pronouncement when the circumstances called for an explanation. To justify his controversial decision suspending the Salt March, during which millions of Indians protested the British salt monopoly through tax strikes and civil resistance, Gandhi simply declared: "It was concluded because it had to be."[19]

Furthermore, it was not only Gandhi's actions that contradicted his words. His statements also, and often

flagrantly, contradicted each other. He could denounce
ad nauseam and in broad strokes modern medical proce-
dures[20] yet still aver that "the West has always commanded
my admiration [for] its surgical inventions and all-round
progress in that direction."[21] He could contend that "in any
examination of moral conduct, the intention is the chief in-
gredient," and simultaneously contend that "a man must
be judged by his action, not the motive prompting it."[22]
He could deplore as a species of violence "a living wall of
pickets in order to prevent the entry of persons into pick-
eted places,"[23] yet at the same time advise an Indian correspondent, whose seat was snatched by a British soldier at
the cinema, that he should "deliberately so to stand as to
obstruct the view of the usurper."[24] He could state in one
breath that even in "the classical instance of the defense-
less sister or mother who is threatened with molestation
by an evil-minded ruffian," resort to violence would not be
justifiable,[25] yet in the next breath "defend" use of violence
"against the whole world if I found myself in a corner when
I could not save a helpless girl from violation."[26]

Gandhi could avow during World War II that his "sympathies are wholly with the Allies" because "this war is resolving itself into one between such democracy as the West
has evolved and totalitarianism as it is typified in Hitler,"
that "There is a fundamental difference between Fascism
and even this [British] imperialism which I am fighting,"
and right after World War II that "a victory for the Axis
would have been far worse. The Axis had accepted violence
as their creed. The Allies had not done so. They at least paid
lip service to peace and freedom, and truth and nonviolence."[27] Yet, he could more or less concurrently avow that
"Hitlerism and Churchillism are in fact the same thing,"

and that "I must fight Nazism and Fascism equally with the enslaving British imperialism."[28] He could praise the decision of French leaders not to resist Nazi aggression because "the cause of liberty becomes a mockery if the price to be paid is wholesale destruction of those who are to enjoy liberty," yet he could also assert that "no greater evil can befall a country than that it should lose its independence,"[29] and that nations occupied by the Nazis should choose annihilation rather than cooperate with the occupiers.[30]

Humble as he indubitably was, Gandhi nonetheless always seemed to believe, mistakenly, that he had bested detractors who pointed out an inconsistency of his. But it must also be said that he never shied away from giving critics of his pronouncements and policies a fair hearing. In conveying an intellectual or political dispute, he did not rig its terms to favor him or create straw men.

If Gandhi was more inconsistent than he let on, it should perhaps also be recalled that Gandhi conceived himself as "essentially a man of action and a reformer," a "practical idealist," "a man of action" for whom "logic comes afterwards, it does not precede the event," and "not built for academic writings. Action is my domain."[31] Intellectual coherence and rigor figured as low priorities compared to getting things done.[32] He accordingly urged interlocutors who detected "inconsistencies, so-called or real" in this or that pronouncement of his to examine each one solely on its own "merits and bless the effort if they can."[33]

While taking note of Gandhi's vacillations, it also bears repeating that his accommodation to circumstance went hand-in-hand with a rare faithfulness to principle. Were he just another pragmatic politician, Gandhi could not have won the devotion of India's impoverished masses. "I claim to be a practical idealist. I believe in compromise." But only, Gandhi qualified, "so long as it does not involve the sacrifice of principles."[34] On one of these core beliefs, truth-telling, Gandhi avowed, "There never can be an occasion when one must tell a lie. If there can be such an occasion, then it would follow that the principle of following truth in speech and action was imperfect. There can be no exception to a principle, and hence there can be no atonement for untruth spoken knowingly."[35] Like everyone else, Gandhi no doubt succumbed to self-deception, but unlike almost anyone else, and corny as it might sound and dubious as it might appear, he probably never consciously lied.

It is not just because of Gandhi's many flip-flops, how-ever, that one is hard-pressed to distill from his life's work a coherent doctrine. He could also be superficial, flippant and downright arrogant. Gandhi passed sweeping verdicts on topics such as socialism, although conceding that "I have read no books on the subject,"[36] and on motion pictures, which he did "not like," although admitting that "I have never gone to a cinema."[37] He could issue statements on behalf of the "All-India Women's Conference" to its British "sisters," and declare before an audience of women that "I know your sex and your needs better than you do your-selves."[38]

Additionally, Gandhi never bothered to produce a systematic handbook on *satyagraha* because, according to him, to "live it" and "practice the idea in my own life" better conveyed its meaning.[39] One has to piece together his doctrine from scattered and not only incongruous but also confusing and obscure fragments.

What confounds yet more, Gandhi blithely conflated categories and collapsed critical distinctions. He made it appear as if he were uniformly applying one simple doctrine, whereas in fact it was a subtly differentiated one. He directed his appeal, depending on the occasion, to qualitatively different audiences. Sometimes he strove to "melt the heart" of the actual malefactor into submission, sometimes he strove to "quicken the conscience" of the passive bystander into action. By the same token, he sought to convert his audience, depending on the occasion, via qualitatively different tactics. Sometimes he used moral suasion, but sometimes he used coercive force, although he subsumed both these tactics under the same, deceptively benign rubric of nonviolence.

What makes a rational account of Gandhi's doctrine most elusive, however, is that it was steeped in religious faith. "It is faith that sustains me," he intoned, "and it is faith that must sustain the other *satyagrahis*"; "The root of *satyagraha* is in prayer." But Gandhi's doctrine was not just born of faith. He also explicitly counterposed it to one grounded in reason: "Faith is not a question of reason. It comes from within"; "My thinking nowadays takes the form exclusively of prayer. I do not use my reason, but look into my heart."[40] Although eager to recruit *satyagrahis* for the struggle, Gandhi was emphatic that communists and other nonbelievers need not apply, because "real love for man I regard to be utterly impossible without love for God."[41]

When Gandhi embarked on a civil disobedience campaign, a fast, or negotiations, it was not—at any rate, not self-consciously—after a material reckoning of the "balance of forces," but instead after an "inner urge," "inner voice," or "gift from God" prompted him. "I am not guided by reason," he avowed, "but by instinct or in other words by the inner voice and one never knows where that voice would lead you to"; "I do not depend upon my intellect to decide upon any action. For me the reasoned course of action is held in check subject to the sanction of the inner voice."[42] It should be obvious that, on such a basis, the movement Gandhi built could not but be authoritarian: How does one argue with an "inner voice"?

Gandhi denoted *satyagraha* a "science,"[43] and conceived it not as a closed system but, in scientific spirit, as ceaseless experimentation in a perpetual and always incomplete search for truth. Still, his was a "science" not amenable to external proof or refutation; its power sprang from the "efficacy of the incalculable force of inscrutable divinity."[44] If *ahimsa* (nonviolence) did not produce the desired outcome, this demonstrated not an inadequacy in the science but an impurity lurking in its human agent: "*Ahimsa* is always infallible. When, therefore, it appears to have failed, the failure is due to the inaptitude of the votary."[45] Gandhi might have been right, but it is hard to figure how one could have proven him wrong, just as one could not answer, because they were literally unanswerable, his Olympian pronouncements and saccharine bromides such as nonviolence, buoyed by the intervention of God, being the most potent force in the world.[46]

In principle Gandhi praised "independent thinking" as the "very essence of the spirit of democracy." He professed, "It is certainly not my wish, nor is it desirable, that everyone who comes close to me should be like me in every respect. That would mean mechanical imitation"; "I do not wish to make everybody like me. My teaching is that everybody should be true to himself"; "I ask no one to follow me. Each should go by the voice within . . . you must on no account blindly follow anybody."[47]

Nonetheless Gandhi asserted a proprietary right over nonviolent resistance because he was the "sole authority on *satyagraha*," "most experienced *satyagrahi*," and "author of *satyagraha* and general in *satyagraha* action."[48] And inasmuch as he was, or conceived himself to be, uniquely privy to the mysteries of *satyagraha*, no one had title to argue with him about it: "I think and feel that it is God within Who is moving me and using me as His instrument"; "I am confident that God has made me the instrument of showing the better way."[49] Put simply, to doubt Gandhi was to doubt God.

If one challenged Gandhi's judgment, it could only be because the skeptic had "superficial knowledge" of *satyagraha*, which furthermore could not be helped "because this philosophy could not be studied from books."[50] And if Gandhi knew better, it was because of his unmatched "achievement based on forty years' experience."[51]

One could march behind Gandhi, or choose not to. One could not, however, decide on a course of action beside yet despite him. Thus he would proclaim, "There is a rule that no one should go on a fast without my permission"; "If we want to work nonviolently, then it is necessary to accept the restrictions laid down by me"; "Anyone whose fast is related to *satyagraha* should seek my permission and obtain it in writing before embarking on it. If this advice is followed, there is no need for framing rules, at any rate, in my lifetime"; "Fasting for a public cause also has its *shastra* [specialized or technical knowledge] and I am the only one adequately versed in it."[52] On other occasions Gandhi counseled his disciples not to fear thinking and acting for themselves, but only because he would be around to correct their errors.[53]

Gandhi eschewed all sectarian "isms," including "Gandhism." "I love to hear the words: 'Down with Gandhism,'" he declared. "An 'ism' deserves to be destroyed."[54] But the alternative he offered often had the feel of autocratic whimsy. Gandhi had a party line not just on sexual abstinence and vegetarianism, but also on "idle jokes" (opposed), "innocent pleasantries" (perhaps), wristwatches (opposed), underwear (opposed), conversing while at work (opposed), and pencils and fountain pens (opposed).[55] He sometimes sounded like Stalin pronouncing on linguistics, albeit in his case deviationists might be banished from his ashram but not deported to the Gulag.[56]

The bottom line is that much of Gandhi's doctrine was inseparable from his person and personality. Still, it was much less arbitrary and much more coherent than he sometimes made it sound.

In any exposition of *satyagraha*, it must also be remembered that Gandhi did not conceive nonviolent resistance as the heart of his doctrine. He situated *satyagraha* in a matrix of daily activities, what he called the "constructive program," that formed the "foundation for civil disobedience." Its planks included expunging from Hinduism the "blot" of untouchability, fostering Hindu-Muslim unity, and promoting use on a mass scale of the spinning wheel (*tcharka*) and handspun cloth (*khadi*).

On this practical basis, Gandhi believed, Indians could forge unbreakable bonds of unbounded love that transcended sect and class. Once Indians adhered to the constructive program, Gandhi further prophesized, complete self-rule (*purna swaraj*) would drop like a ripe fruit into India's lap and political confrontation with Great Britain would be unnecessary, while the nonviolent future of India would be safeguarded: "If we learn to love one another, if the gulf between Hindu and Muslim, caste and outcaste, and rich and poor is obliterated, a handful of English would not dare to continue their rule over us."[57]

In conclusion, it must be conceded that Gandhi would almost certainly have questioned my goal in writing this book. He was firmly wedded to the belief that a rational core of *satyagraha* could not be separated out from its spiritual essence: "It is impossible that a thing essentially of the soul can be imparted through the intellect."[58]

I am nonetheless convinced that Gandhi has important things to say on the subject of nonviolent resistance, from which even the most resolute secularist would greatly benefit, and that the content of his doctrine can be accessed by reason and made accessible to the rational mind. It will be for the reader to decide whether I am right.

2/ DEATH PILLOW

What is *satyagraha*?

The "votaries" of nonviolent civil resistance, according to Gandhi, have to purge themselves of any and all aggressive impulses. They "must not be violent in thought, word or deed," in fact, must be "incapable of feeling or harboring anger."[1]

The essence of Gandhi's creed is not, however, a negative "non"-principle but the affirmative or "active" principle of "unadulterated love—fellow-feeling," which in turn springs from "faith in the inherent goodness of human nature," and the belief that "what holds good in respect of yourself holds good equally in respect of the whole universe. All mankind in essence are alike."[2] If even one person is unimpeachably loving and good, then we all are.

True, the annals of humankind appear rife with violence. But, Gandhi contended, this was an optical illusion fostered by scribes and scholars who, by virtue of their profession, took note of the exceptions to the rule: "History is really a record of every interruption of the even working of the force of love or of the soul."[3]

"The law of love," Gandhi professed, "rules mankind." Were it otherwise, we would not still be around: "The fact that mankind persists shows that the cohesive force is greater than the disruptive force, centripetal force greater than centrifugal"; "Had violence, i.e., hate, ruled us, we should have become extinct long ago"; "If the sum-total of the world's activities was destructive, it would have come to an end long ago."[4]

Just as "families or even clans" manage to resolve conflicts nonviolently through the binding powers of love, so can "humankind," which is "one big family."[5] To illustrate love's power to overcome violent tyranny, Gandhi often pointed to the metamorphosis in his own spousal relations: although "I literally used to make life a hell for her," eventually "her guileless simplicity conquered me completely."[6]

Gandhi's faith in the inherent goodness of humankind could stretch credulity to its limits. In 1940 he wrote a "Dear Friend" letter to Hitler in which he averred *not* "to believe that you are the monster described by your opponents," albeit acknowledging that "many of your acts are monstrous and unbecoming of human dignity."[7]

Because love is at its core, *satyagraha* eschews violence. It also eschews inflicting indirect, non-physical, quasi forms of coercion such as fear, lying, and embarrassment.[8] Gandhi additionally denounced assaults on property or even scaling walls enclosing private property as "pure violence."[9]

Unlike violence, which "obtains reforms by external means," *satyagraha*, according to Gandhi, relied exclusively on the internal method of "self-purification" that came of self-suffering: "the more innocent and pure the suffering the more potent will it be in its effect."[10] The purpose of such self-sacrifice was to arouse from its slumber the conscience of wrongdoers in order "to convert, not to coerce" them, and the conscience of sympathetic bystanders in order to galvanize them into action.[11]

The greater the number of *satyagrahis* ready to sacrifice themselves, and the more unalloyed their motives, Gandhi declared during the Salt March, the sooner victory would be theirs: "Unless thousands die, *swaraj* [independence] . . . will not be secured. The purer the men sacrificing themselves in this cause, the earlier shall we get *swaraj* and the less will be the number of people sacrificed"; "Nothing will be better than if this band of *satyagrahis* perishes."[12] A *satyagrahi*'s ultimate sacrifice, according to Gandhi, not only pricked the public's conscience but also "purifies those left behind and awakens a greater spirit of service."[13] In another version, he pointed to the transforming powers not of self-suffering per se but of the "upwelling of love and pity towards the wrongdoer."[14]

Gandhi censured resort to violence on both personal and political, and both moral and pragmatic, grounds. It corrupted the individual, who was degraded to the level of a beast: "That which distinguishes man from all other animals is his capacity to be nonviolent."[15] But it also tainted the goal of an enlightened politics. Means and ends, he suggested in an evocative simile, were inextricably intertwined: "The means may be likened to a seed, the end to a tree." Consequently, however just the cause, the resort to violence as a political weapon would always and inevitably place the "powerful and mighty" at the apex of a hierarchy, while the "blind, the halt and the maimed" remain disenfranchised: "violence may destroy one or more bad rulers, but . . . others will pop up in their places."[16]

Gandhi further contended that any victory achieved through violence would be fleeting: "a man who yields to threat or physical coercion resents it and simply awaits a suitable opportunity to revert to his original ways and resorts to reprisals when he is able to exact them."[17]

The recourse to violent means also excluded from political participation those unwilling or unable to wield it, but without whom the struggle could not be won:

> Do you think that all the women and the children who covered themselves with glory during the last campaign [Salt March] would have done so if we had pursued the path of violence? Would they have been here today? Would our women, known as the meekest on earth, would women like Gangabehn, who stood the *lathi*-blows until her white sari was drenched in blood, have done the unique service they did if we had violence in us? With God's name on their lips, she and her sisters hurled defiance at their oppressors, without anger in their hearts. And our children—our *vanarasena* (monkey-army). How could you have had these innocent ones, who renounced their toys, their kites and their crackers, and joined as soldiers of *swaraj*—how could you have enlisted them in a violent struggle? We were able to enlist as soldiers millions of men, women and children because we were pledged to nonviolence.[18]

On other occasions Gandhi would pragmatically argue that, whereas violence was perhaps a viable option elsewhere, "terrorism is the very worst thing for India in a special manner, because India is a foreign soil for terrorism to flourish in."[19]

Even, or especially, in the face of the ruthless Axis aggression during World War II, according to Gandhi, the use of armed force was to be eschewed. If the Allies did manage to inflict a military defeat on the Axis, it could only be by becoming "stronger than they are, and therefore worse and more ruthless"; "that would mean no deliverance from Nazism," but "superior Nazism."[20] Victor would come to resemble, and consequently would in effect *be*, vanquished, while "such a victory must mean another preparation for a war more inhuman than the present, as this one had proved more inhuman than the last."[21]

On many counts Gandhi's diagnosis and prognosis appear wanting. Although committing many atrocities, the Allied states coming out of World War II did not mirror, let alone surpass, Nazi Germany in brutality. Nonetheless, even after the war ended, Gandhi was unrepentant on this point: "the United Nations set out to fight Hitler with his weapons and ended by out-Hitlering Hitler"; "what had happened in Europe was that Hitlerism had only been destroyed by super-Hitlerism"; "whilst the enemy powers so-called were crushed, the Allied Powers had won but an empty victory. Apart from the wanton destruction of human heads, they had—between the Allies and the enemies—succeeded in draining the world of its food materials and cloth. And the former seemed to be so dehumanized that they had entertained the vain hope of reducing the enemies to helotry. It was a question whom to pity more—the Allies or the enemies."[22]

In addition Gandhi posited that nonviolent resistance could not produce inferior results to violent resistance. "Either the enemy comes to terms with you, then you win without blood," he reasoned, "or the enemy annihilates you. This last solution is not worse than what a violent war in any case brings about."[23] Gandhi willfully ignored the third possibility that violent resistance could defeat the Nazis short of one's annihilation, albeit at a terrible human cost, which is, of course, what happened. It is more difficult to gainsay Gandhi's assertion that, once having imitated Nazi methods, a cause "cannot be called just,"[24] except to conjure up pedantic and morally obtuse distinctions between Auschwitz and Hiroshima.

But, however much he deplored violence, Gandhi did not unreservedly oppose it.[25] In the first place, he did not categorize forceful resistance in the face of impossible odds—a woman fending off a rapist with her bare hands, an unarmed man resisting torture by a gang, Polish armed self-defense in the face of the Nazi aggression—as violence. In his reckoning such resort to force was largely symbolic and instinctive, akin to the "struggling of a mouse against a cat." In the instance of a rape victim, her "slap or scratching" manifested the "resolve" to "offer up . . . body and life, but . . . not become a coward. . . . It is in itself an act of non-violence. She has no strength to cause harm"; the "slap rouses oneself, makes oneself fearless and above all, gives oneself the strength to die."[26]

Furthermore, until and unless he converted others to his beliefs, Gandhi accepted that only the prevailing moral-legal norms bound the actions of individuals. Thus, while personally renouncing it, he did acknowledge the legitimacy of resort to violence in a righteous cause: "self-defense is everybody's birthright."[27]

In the face of personal insult and "if you feel humiliated," Gandhi opined, sounding more like Malcolm X than Martin Luther King, "you will be justified in slapping the bully in the face or taking whatever action you might deem necessary to vindicate your self-respect."[28] And although "not defending the Arab excesses" during the 1936–1939 Arab Revolt in Palestine, and although "wishing they had chosen the way of nonviolence in resisting what they rightly regarded as an unwarrantable encroachment upon their country," Gandhi nonetheless maintained that "according to the accepted canons of right and wrong, nothing can be said against the Arab resistance in the face of overwhelming odds."[29]

GANDHI AND PALESTINE

Gandhi rejected the ideological tenets underpinning the Zionist colonization of Palestine. He did not accept that Jews had a biblical title to Palestine, and instead counseled them to seek their rights in the countries where they resided. If Jews did decide to go to Palestine, it had to be with the consent of the indigenous population. Otherwise, "they are co-sharers with the British in despoiling a people who have done no wrong to them."[30] Late in life Gandhi was seemingly less critical of the Jews' aspiration to settle in Palestine, but he still deplored that they were "seeking to impose themselves on Palestine with the aid of America and Britain and now with the aid of naked terrorism."[31] A cottage industry has sprung up trying to prove that what Gandhi repeatedly said on Palestine and Zionism he did not really mean.[32] The scholarly output is long on speculation and rich in digression, but precious short on substantiating evidence.

On comparable grounds, although personally opposing "punishment" for lawbreakers because it was a species of violence, Gandhi still acquiesced in the practice because "governments functioning today are based on the theory of punishment." He even appeared to sanction shooting those guilty of treason because "Everywhere in the world traitors are shot down as a rule."[33]

But Gandhi did not just extenuate violence on circum-stantial grounds.[34] He also positively *advocated* it if, in the face of an injustice, the only other options were abject surrender or retreat. Gandhi detested "mute submissive-ness"[35] more than violence and, what was yet more sinful in his eyes, such subjection masquerading as nonviolent resistance. Should one be incapable of nonviolently resist-ing an outrage, then the only honorable recourse would be to resist violently, whereas flight would be wholly shameful.

Gandhi ranked not violence but pusillanimity and effeminacy as the worst personal failings and the most egregious "shortcoming" of Indians, while he prized the qualities of courage and manliness: "nonviolence is the greatest virtue, cowardice the greatest vice"; "the funda-mental thing to be borne in mind is that people should, under no circumstances, be cowardly or impotent"; "it is unmanly to run away from danger."[36] Gandhi tersely defined the "aim of the *satyagraha* struggle" he led in South Africa as being "to infuse manliness in cowards."[37]

Ironically, on the very rare occasions when Gandhi used brutal language, he directed it not at those who practiced violence but instead at those who feared it: "Cowardice is impotence worse than violence. The coward desires revenge but being afraid to die, he looks to others, maybe the Government of the day, to do the work of defense for him. *A coward is less than a man. He does not deserve to be a member of a society of men and women*"; "[Those who] continued to look to the police and the military for help . . . would remain slaves for ever. Those who preferred security to freedom *had no right to live*."[38] One who refrained from shedding blood because of fear effectively stood lower on Gandhi's moral hierarchy than one who would shed it in bucket loads. Indeed, in his moral calculus, cowardice constituted the ultimate manifestation of violence: "Doing injury to another is obviously violence, but harboring injury to another and yet unwillingness from cowardice to defend oneself or one's neighbor is also violence, and probably worse than the first."[39]

If Gandhi despised one thing more than cowardice, it was cowardice wrapping itself in the mantle of non-violence. He was emphatic that if one could not summon the inner resources to be nonviolent, then forceful retaliation was not only justified but also imperative, while flight in the name of nonviolence was contemptible. Gandhi's collected works are filled with, on the one hand, scalding condemnations of ersatz nonviolence and, on the other, exhortations to violence if the only other option is craven retreat. Strangely, they echo and recall the imagery of Nietzsche's acid critique of Christian "slave morality" that inverts weakness into a virtue while devaluing courage and strength. Consider the representative passages below.

I Can Only Prefer Violence to Cowardice

1920	1924
Where there is only a choice between cowardice and violence, I would advise violence. Thus when my eldest son asked me what he should have done, had he been present when I was almost fatally assaulted in 1908, whether he should have run away and seen me killed or whether he should have used his physical force, which he could and wanted to use, and defended me, I told him that it was his duty to defend me even by using violence.... Hence ... I advocate training in arms for those who believe in the method of violence. I would rather have India resort to arms in order to defend her honor than that she should in a cowardly manner become or remain a helpless witness to her own dishonor. But I believe that nonviolence is infinitely superior to violence, forgiveness is more manly than punishment.... But abstinence is forgiveness only when there is the power to punish; it is meaningless where it pretends to proceed from a helpless creature. A mouse hardly forgives a cat when it allows itself to be torn to pieces by her.[40]	My nonviolence does not admit of running away from danger and leaving dear ones unprotected. Between violence and cowardly flight, I can only prefer violence to cowardice. I can no more preach nonviolence to a coward than I can tempt a blind man to enjoy healthy scenes. Nonviolence is the summit of bravery. And in my own experience, I have had no difficulty in demonstrating to men trained in the school of violence the superiority of nonviolence. As a coward, which I was for years, I harbored violence. I began to prize nonviolence only when I began to shed cowardice. Those Hindus who ran away from the post of duty when it was attended with danger did so not because they were nonviolent, or because they were afraid to strike, but because they were unwilling to die or even suffer any injury. A rabbit that runs away from the bull terrier is not particularly nonviolent. The poor thing trembles at the sight of the terrier and runs for very life. Those Hindus who ran away to save their lives would have been truly nonviolent and would have covered themselves with glory and added luster to their faith and won the friendship of their Mussalman assailants, if they had stood bare breast with smiles on their lips, and died at their post. They would have done less well, though still well, if they had stood at these posts and returned blow for blow. If the Hindus wish to convert the Mussalman bully into a respecting friend, they have to learn to die in the face of the heaviest odds.[41]

I Can Only Prefer Violence to Cowardice

1935	1939

Nonviolence cannot be taught to a person who fears to die and has no power of resistance. A helpless mouse is not nonviolent because he is always eaten by [a] pussy[cat]. He would gladly eat the murderess if he could, but he ever tries to flee from her. We do not call him a coward, because he is made by nature to behave no better than he does. But a man who, when faced by danger, behaves like a mouse, is rightly called a coward. He harbors violence and hatred in his heart and would kill his enemy if he could without being hurt himself. He is a stranger to nonviolence. All sermonizing on it will be lost on him. Bravery is foreign to his nature. Before he can understand nonviolence he has to be taught to stand his ground and even suffer death in the attempt to defend himself against the aggressor who bids fair to overwhelm him. To do otherwise would be to confirm his cowardice and take him further away from nonviolence. Whilst I may not actually help anyone to retaliate, I must not let a coward seek shelter behind nonviolence so-called. Not knowing the stuff of which nonviolence is made many have honestly believed that running away from danger every time was a virtue compared to offering resistance, especially when it is fraught with danger to one's life. As a teacher of nonviolence I must, so far as it is possible for me, guard against such an unmanly belief.... Self-defense ... is the only honorable course where there is unreadiness for self-immolation.[42]

For I cannot in any case stand cowardice. Let no one say when I am gone that I taught the people to be cowards. If you think my *ahimsa* amounts to that, or leads you to that, you should reject it without hesitation. I would far rather that you died bravely dealing a blow and receiving a blow than died in abject terror.... Fleeing from battle ... is cowardice, and unworthy of a warrior. An armed fighter is known to have sought fresh arms as soon as he loses those in his possession or they lose their efficacy. He leaves the battle to get them. A nonviolent warrior knows no leaving the battle. He rushes into the mouth of *himsa* [violence], never even once harboring an evil thought. If this *ahimsa* seems to you to be impossible, let us be honest with ourselves and say so, and give it up.... Cowardice is worse than violence because cowards can never be nonviolent. So such people should learn to defend themselves.... A person who has full faith in nonviolence should be a thousand times more fearless than an armed man.... It is the duty of every believer in *ahimsa* to see that cowardice is not propagated in the name of nonviolence.[43]

These passages, which span the gamut of Gandhi's public life, strike identical chords: nonviolence born of fear is cowardice; cowardice is worse than violence; violent retaliation is morally superior to fear-inspired abstention.

The authentic spirit of nonviolence and the warrior spirit, Gandhi paradoxically suggested, both sprang from the identical source: fearlessness. He heaped praise on the "reckless courage" of soldiers on the battlefield, and wanted "to learn . . . the art of throwing away my life for a noble cause."[44] He held up the "example of Sparta," because "though they were an armed people and also few, they laid down their lives but would not leave their places."[45] He drew inspiration from the typical "Pathan [Pashtun] boy" because he is "fearless. If there is bloodshed he does not hide himself in his house. He finds pleasure in fighting. He does not stop to think that he might be injured or even killed. He is never afraid of being hurt. I have seen one standing unmoved in the midst of blood gushing from his many wounds."[46]

Inversely, Gandhi chastised (albeit mistakenly) German Jews for pretending to nonviolence yet seeking violent revenge on the Nazis: "There is no nonviolence in their hearts. Their nonviolence, if it may be so called, is of the helpless and the weak."[47] Likewise, Gandhi rebuked the cowardice of his disciples who elected milder, to evade severer, sanctions: "The nonviolence of the person who went to jail to avoid a worse fate harmed him and disgraced the cause which he used as a shelter to escape death."[48]

But Gandhi also candidly confessed his own failure to meet the heroic standard he set.[49] He attributed this gap between ideal and practice to his intellectual acceptance of death but his emotional recoiling from it.[50] Still, in the last year of his life Gandhi seemingly wanted to die at his post. Because he wanted to demonstrate in his own person that it was possible to court death consciously and to accept it serenely. Because he believed that "the greatest bravery lies in having the courage to die."[51] And because he had dispatched so many of his disciples to their deaths, and even demanded of them that they get themselves killed, during the inter-communal fighting. In response to local leaders who solicited his advice on how to end the internecine bloodletting, Gandhi counseled: "Go in the midst of the rioters and prevent them from indulging in madness or get killed in the attempt. But do not come back alive to report failure. The situation calls for sacrifice on the part of top-rankers."[52]

While enthralled by battlefield heroics, Gandhi professed that the *satyagrahi* had to bring forth yet greater reserves of inner courage than the armed combatant: "I believe that a man is the strongest soldier for daring to die unarmed with his breast bare before the enemy"; "To die without killing requires more heroism. There is nothing very wonderful in killing and being killed in the process. But the man who offers his neck to the enemy for execution but refuses to bend to his will shows courage of a far higher type."[53]

It was incumbent upon *satyagrahis* to accept, indeed relish, the prospect of mutely subjecting themselves to mass slaughter. "Such an army should be ready to cope with any emergency," Gandhi declared amid inter-communal fighting, "and in order to still the frenzy of mobs, should risk their lives in numbers sufficient for the purpose. A few hundred, maybe a few thousand, such spotless deaths will once and for all put an end to the riots." And they must not draw back from the fate awaiting them: "if we are to train ourselves to receive the bullet wounds or bayonet charges in our bare chests, we must accustom ourselves to standing unmoved in the face of cavalry or baton charges."[54]

In stirring phrases Gandhi called upon his disciples to march headlong, unarmed yet "smilingly" and "cheerfully," into the valley of death, while earnestly praying, "May good befall him who kills me!"[55] He posited that the more one internalized the true spirit of nonviolence born of fearlessness, the less inclined one would be to exact revenge: "When a man is fully ready to die he will not even desire to offer violence . . . the desire to kill is in inverse proportion to the desire to die."[56] Of which, it might be said, Gandhi's own death was exemplary.

"Wherein is courage required," Gandhi rhetorically asked, "in blowing others to pieces from behind a cannon, or with a smiling face to approach a cannon and to be blown to pieces? Who is the true warrior—he who keeps death always as a bosom-friend or he who controls the death of others?"[57] "What I shall expect of you," he lectured the "officers" of his army, "is that even if someone subjects you to the most inhuman tortures, you will joyfully face the ordeal and make the supreme sacrifice with God's name on your lips and without a trace of fear or anger or thoughts of revenge in your hearts."[58] And in a macabre peroration, he avowed, "That nation is great which rests its head upon death as its pillow."[59]

It might fairly be said that Gandhi fostered a death cult. Consider the representative passages assembled below. His cavalier indifference to life and morbid embrace of death are the most unappealing and incoherent facets of his doctrine.

It Would Exhilarate Me to Hear That a Coworker Was Shot Dead

Whilst therefore I tender my sympathy to the parents of the two brave lads who lost their lives [he said after the murder of these disciples], my inmost desire is to congratulate them for the finished sacrifices of their sons, if they would accept my congratulations. A warrior's death is never a matter of sorrow, still less that of a *satyagrahi* warrior. One of the lessons that a nation yearning for freedom needs to learn is to shed several fears; fear of losing title, wealth, position, fear of imprisonment, of bodily injury and lastly of death.[60]

I attach no value now to jail-going. I feel no exhilaration when I hear that some coworker of mine was sentenced to one year or two years, or, for that matter, even five years. It would exhilarate me to hear that a coworker like Jairamdas was shot dead or that another coworker, of an equally spotless character, had had his skull broken.... If Ramniklal had made an offering of his head and a patch of Bulsar land had been besmeared with his blood, then you would have been justified in asking me to come.... Such heroism is being displayed at Anand and at Dehwan. There volunteers were beaten up in the night and, so that the police might enjoy beating them, lights were put out. If they call me there, I would immediately go. There is an occasion worth celebrating.[61]

Two Hindu workers and a Muslim worker set out to quell the riots and died in the effort. I am not unhappy at their death. I do not weep for them. Ganesh Shankar Vidyarthi laid down his life similarly in the Kanpur riots.... I was happy at his death. I do not say all this to excite you. I want to make you understand that if you but learn how to die all will be well.[62]

Gandhi would even balk at extending condolences on receipt of a death notice. (See the columns below for Gandhi's typical acknowledgments.) Instead, he waxed philosophical that birth and death are inevitable and complementary stages in nature's cycle, "one and the same thing."[63] Far from being cause for sorrow or dread, death for

Gandhi was "a necessary and beneficial phenomenon," "a deliverance," "that inevitable and grand event," a "boon," "a friend. What would we have done if there were no Death?"[64]

WHY GRIEVE OVER ANYONE'S DEATH?

There is not the slightest reason to be grieved by the death of friends. None ever dies before his time. The notion of untimely death is a delusion. Even the death of a day-old baby is not an untimely one. It only means that the actions to be performed through that body had been performed. We feel pained by death only because of our ignorance and selfishness. We feel agitated over the death of friends or others because of our ignorance of the soul's attributes and because we do not wish ourselves to die.[65]

Why do you feel so unhappy? After all, no great tragedy has struck you down. There is no law that no one shall die young. Moreover, you and I have not one child, but countless children. Some of them will die and others will be born to take their place. Why, then, keep count of who dies and who lives?[66]

To mourn the death of either son or husband is meaningless and shows our ignorance. This should not be dismissed as merely wise talk; it is a truth to be pondered over till it sinks into our heart and to be acted upon. Since death is certain for all, the only question is whether it comes today or tomorrow. Why, then, should we grieve over anyone's death? It is only the body which dies. That is its nature and therefore there is no cause for wonder when it dies. It is certain that the soul which dwells in the body never dies, it is immortal. When we know this as certain truth, why should we grieve over death?[67]

If Gandhi truly believed this, and there seems no reason not to take him at his word, it forces one to wonder why he considered nonviolence so sacred a calling: by his reckoning, to kill someone is just not such a big deal. Furthermore, if life and death are mere ephemera in nature's eternal cycle, why should a *satyagrahi*'s willingness to die prick anyone's conscience, and why should it be judged heroic if a *satyagrahi* wills his death?

The ideal *satyagrahi*, according to Gandhi, marches smilingly and cheerfully into the line of fire and gets blown to pieces. But, then, the *satyagrahi* most resembles the member of a crazed cult or the mentally unhinged. True, beholding such a sight might move the public to feel revulsion, but it is hard to conceive how such a death will inspire *respect* for the victim.

Isn't it the fact that a person who stands poised to make the supreme sacrifice for an ideal *also and concurrently* clings to life and, if not absolutely dreading death, still *loves life*—and not just loves life because it enables one to sacrifice it, which is how Gandhi conceived life—isn't it *that* fact that causes the rest of humanity to honor martyrs and moves our consciences at their untimely and unjust passing?

Gandhi so devalues life that life and death truly become indistinguishable, and seeking to preserve life, let alone at the ultimate price of self-immolation, becomes a contradiction in terms. Why sacrifice one's own life for the sake of others if it is, or should be, a matter of indifference whether they are dead or alive?

It is also hard to fathom why Gandhi should feel "exhilaration" at a *satyagrahi*'s violent death or the smashing of his skull. To give one's life for a just cause is surely deserving of the highest respect but it merits such admiration precisely because it is a *sacrifice*—because life is so worth living and we all do, or should, want to live. Isn't the proper acknowledgment of such martyrdom not elation but *awe* at the human capacity to act out such devotion to an ideal as well as *mourning* for a life that missed out on the joy of *living* it to the fullest? If pathos and poignancy attach to martyrdom, it can only be because of the reverence we attach to life.

Beyond its shamefulness, Gandhi rejected nonviolence born of weakness because it was politically ineffectual. If the votaries of nonviolence abjured violence only from fear of retaliation, then the wrongdoer had every right to dread what might ensue should they attain power and control the levers of repression, and therefore had every incentive to resist unto the death a handing over of power.

In order to convince the wrongdoer that one's non-violence was not born of weakness, and hence that the wrongdoer had nothing to fear if the tables were turned, *satyagrahis* needed to demonstrate—make manifest—the willingness to forego violence even when they did *not* fear violent retaliation. One such scenario would be if those practicing nonviolence vastly outnumbered and could easily overwhelm the wrongdoer, but chose not to.

The nonviolence of "India as a nation . . . is that of the weak," Gandhi lamented. "If she were nonviolent in the consciousness of her strength, Englishmen would lose their role of distrustful conquerors. . . . If we, as Indians, could but for a moment visualize ourselves as a strong people disdaining to strike, we should cease to fear Englishmen whether as soldiers, traders or administrators, and they to distrust us."[68] And again: "The moment Englishmen feel that although they are in India in a hopeless minority, their lives are protected against harm not because of the match-less weapons of destruction which are at their disposal, but because Indians refuse to take the lives even of those whom they may consider to be utterly in the wrong, that moment will see a transformation in the English nation in its rela-tion to India."[69]

Yet, real-life circumstances often preclude the practical demonstration of a truly nonviolent spirit. How for example could the skeletal inmates of a concentration camp, depleted of any capacity to resist, let alone a capacity to overpower the wrongdoers, make manifest that, if roles were reversed, they would not exact revenge? To be sure, it might be argued in Gandhi's defense that, if nonviolence is to work, it cannot suddenly be invoked when a struggle has already passed the point of no return.

One might also notice in the passages just quoted Gandhi's naïve premise that the fundamental barrier dividing British and Indians was psychological ("fear" and "distrust") and not a material clash of interests. On other occasions he speculated that the British opposed Indian independence because of "the great ignorance that prevails in England about India. Many of the best Englishmen believe that we are incapable of defending ourselves or managing our Finance."[70]

In practice, however, Gandhi harbored few illusions that the antagonistic relationship and consequent British resort to force sprang from brutal exploitation, while the British decision whether to stay or leave would ultimately be decided, not by winning their trust, but by their cold calculation of the bottom line.

3/ QUICKENED CONSCIENCE

How does *satyagraha* work?

Gandhi professed that *satyagraha* was not just non-violent but also noncoercive. In reality, his civil resistance campaigns combined varying degrees of abnegation and coercion.[1]

At one pole was a tactic such as fasting, which manifest-ly contained a large component of self-suffering, but which could also be coercive. Gandhi's defense of public-spirited fasts as purely noncoercive does not convince.

Gandhi posited a distinction between selfless fasts aimed at benefiting others (noncoercive) versus selfish fasts aimed at benefiting one's self (coercive). Some instances would appear to be fairly straightforward: a father who fasts to dissuade his son from snorting cocaine versus a son who fasts to persuade his father to buy him a BMW.

But in real life it is not so simple. If the alleged wrong-doer does not concur on the legitimacy of the faster's goal, he will surely *experience* the fast as coercive even if the faster conceives it as a beneficent act.

When late in life Gandhi slept naked with young girls to test his capacity for sexual restraint, many of his associates were appalled to the point of breaking off relations with him. Gandhi dubbed their severance of ties a form of "noncooperation with me," and was deeply troubled by the loss. Nonetheless, he insisted that he had done no wrong, indeed, that his religious faith compelled him along his chosen path. If they had gone one step further and fasted in protest and to awaken his conscience, would theirs have been a noncoercive or coercive act?

In the absence of a shared moral consensus between the fasting "penitent" and the alleged wrongdoer, the fast will always be subjectively felt by its target as coercive and—for all anyone knows and can know—it also would be, on Gandhi's own terms, objectively coercive. Who's to say, definitively, whether or not the faster's goal is desirable?

Gandhi himself acknowledged that, however sincere, the faster might be wrongly motivated and hence morally culpable, and also that only a thin line might separate selfless from selfish goals. After his imprisonment for protesting the salt tax Gandhi went on a fast because the British denied him permission to see, and thereby also to provide aid and comfort to, his ailing comrades. "The deprivation of touch with these fellow-prisoners," he pled, "is unbearable for me." Was his a selfish or selfless fast?

Gandhi declared that, if in his "ignorance" he might "try through a fast to make the nation agree to an improper demand, I am sure that the nation ought not to yield to such a demand merely for sparing my life, no matter how much

it is convinced of my services to it in the past." Likewise, he
avowed, no doubt sincerely, that "my contemplated fast . . .
is in no way intended to deflect anyone from what he be-
lieves is the course of duty for him." But isn't it more likely
that others would give ground, even if he was in the wrong,
because they wouldn't want the Mahatma to suffer or die?
Despite himself, his fast *would* coerce.

In the hands of a revered but still flawed public figure,
the weapon of a fast can, in other words, easily lend itself
to abuse. Gandhi's fallback defense that one must trust the
judgment of an experienced *satyagrahi* such as himself
scarcely helped. The fact that he occasionally approved of
fasts that, although politically irreproachable, were nonetheless self-interested also muddied the waters. Thus, he
allowed that "under certain circumstances it is permissible
to fast for an increase in wages on behalf of one's group,"
and that "if, in spite of the collections of food grains in the
depot, the hungry cannot get it, . . . they can go on a fast
unto death and thus secure relief for themselves and for
others." What happened to his stricture that one must not
personally benefit from a fast?

Gandhi also purported that moving someone to act (or
not act) as the result of a public fast is no more coercive
than someone being moved to act (or not act) by the "love
of Jesus" or the love of family and friends. But in the face of
sinful temptation, the private voice of one's conscience
admonishing to "do the right thing," is of a different quality
from the coercion of a public spectacle that, whatever the
faster's intention, inevitably carries injury to the object of
the fast. To act out of love for Jesus registers the triumph of
one's moral faculty over less ennobling impulses, whereas
if one succumbs to the external pressure of a fast, it might

just be because of vanity and fear of earthly loss. Thus, when tempted by infidelity, the "higher" voice of conscience curbs one's carnal desires. But if a spouse in the know decides to fast, it might quicken the would-be adulterer's conscience, or it might just quicken his embarrassment at being caught, and his dread of being publicly humiliated and losing conjugal rights.[2]

If fasting stood at one pole of *satyagraha*, at the other extreme was what Gandhi called "noncooperation" such as a general strike, which he in principle supported,[3] although it obstructed society's functioning.[4] Such a tactic was manifestly coercive, yet insofar as the participant faced the loss of a paycheck, punitive sanctions, even internment and death, noncooperation also entailed varying degrees of self-suffering.[5]

To blunt its coercive edge, Gandhi stressed that even noncooperation "must have its roots in love. Its object should not be to punish the opponent or to inflict injury upon him. . . . we must make him feel that in us he has a friend and we should try to reach his heart." And again: "We do want to paralyze the Government considered as a system—not, however, by intimidation, but by the irre-sistible pressure of our innocence."[6] He did allow that, as a "practical" matter, even if noncooperation sprang from the "nonviolence of the weak,"[7] i.e., not from love of the exploiters but from fear that a violent assault on them would provoke yet more violent retribution, it could still be effective "if a sufficient number of people practice it."[8] But Gandhi stubbornly refused to concede that, although love and innocence might lower the temperature of a heated labor struggle, coercion remained the overriding factor at play in noncooperation.[9]

Between the self-suffering of a fast and the coercive force of a strike, Gandhi's other tactics occupied a middle ground. He advocated various forms of civil disobedience, such as nonpayment of taxes, that contained equal parts coerciveness (depriving the state of needed revenues, undermining the rule of law) and self-suffering (going to jail, paying punitive fines), and various forms of civil resistance, the coerciveness of which ranged from more ("political" boycotts targeting goods produced by another country) to less ("unaggressive" picketing).[10]

Finally, it merits mentioning one potent if latent form of violence lurking in the background of Gandhi's activities, of which he was fully cognizant and which he was not averse to exploiting. If the British did not acquiesce in his nonviolent demands, then they would have to cope with wholesale violent resistance instead. "I have claimed in private correspondence with English friends," Gandhi noted, "that it is because of my incessant preaching of the gospel of nonviolence and my having successfully demonstrated its practical utility that so far the forces of violence, which are undoubtedly in existence . . ., have remained under complete control."[11] On the other hand, there is no reason to doubt that Gandhi was sincere in his oft-stated belief that the resort of Indians to violence and terrorism would ultimately harm the cause of Indian independence.[12]

☙❧

The essence of Gandhi's creed was the transformative power of pristine self-suffering. He believed that such suffering would put on display the "human dignity" of the victim and thereby "quicken into life" the public's "sluggish conscience," "awaken the life" of the "sleeping conscience," "quicken the dead conscience into life," "make people think and act," strike a "sympathetic chord," "stir us out of our complacency," and "evoke by his truth and love expressed through his suffering" the "inherent goodness of human nature."

"The world is touched by sacrifice," Gandhi proclaimed. "It can tame the wildest beast, certainly the wildest man," it compels "public opinion . . . to desist from the hypocrisy which is eating into them."[13]

Once having aroused public opinion from its listless-ness, the *satyagrahi* would then be well-placed to "mo-bilize" it "against the evil which he is out to eradicate, by means of a wide and intensive agitation," while his "success is the certain result of suffering of the extremist character, voluntarily undergone."[14]

It is not clear, however, why suffering in and of itself or, for that matter, allied with "love," would galvanize the by-stander, let alone convert the alleged wrongdoer. Were the "pro-life" half of the American population to converge on abortion clinics and pledge a collective fast unto the death until and unless the clinics ceased performing abortions, the "pro-choice" half would almost certainly not be con-verted by such a spectacle.

In other words, it is not suffering alone that touches but suffering *in the pursuit of a legitimate goal*. The public's recognition of the legitimacy of such a goal presumes, however, a preexisting broad consensus, if only latent or incipient, according to which the victims justly deserve what they seek.

When Gandhi referred to the victim's "innocence,"[15] it was in effect, although he didn't always specify it, inno-cence in a double sense: of means—while willing to endure

pain, the victim refrains from inflicting pain on others—
and of *ends*—the victim seeks a right that cannot in good
conscience be denied because it resonates with the "nor-
mal moral sense of the world."[16] "I rely for success," Gandhi
explained, "upon the inherent justice of the national cause
and the equally just means adopted for its vindication."[17]

If the "weapon" of *satyagraha* "depends for success
upon the gathering of public opinion,"[18] then, the more in-
controvertible the ends, the more self-suffering as a means
will spur "enlightened public opinion" into action.[19] But inversely, self-suffering will not pierce the emotional armor
of wrongdoers who are convinced, either due to inimical
interest or inimical ideology or, what's often the case, both
conjoined, that the demands of the victim lack justice. The
spectacle of martyrdom might induce some degree of pity
but, in and of itself, it won't induce those profiting from a
system and convinced of its justice to make major conces-
sions.

Gandhi himself conceded that his interlocutors might
be as convinced in the rightness of their opinions as he was
of his own ("I realize what may appear to me prejudice may
be enlightenment to others"),[20] and that he had to be open
to the possibility that his interlocutors might be right and
he himself wrong ("Nobody in this world possesses abso-
lute truth. This is God's attribute alone. Relative truth is all
we know").[21] But why then would or should the (alleged)
wrongdoer be converted by the self-sacrifice of those pursuing a goal, the justice of which is concededly dubious?

Unlike when violence is brought into play, Gandhi
rightly observed, if the goal turns out to be off the mark, the
satyagrahi's suffering will not have caused bodily harm to
the unfairly targeted wrongdoer: "He does not make others

suffer for his mistakes."[22] But it is also a fact that the wrong-doer's hardened self-interest conveniently packaged in righteous ideology will almost certainly stifle the voice of justice and trump the urgings of pity, thereby nullifying the power of nonviolence.

The point I am making here finds vivid illustration in this passage from Gandhi: "Our triumph consists in thousands being led to the prisons like lambs to the slaughter-house. If the lambs of the world had been willingly led, they would have long ago saved themselves from the butcher's knife. Our triumph consists again in being imprisoned for no wrong whatsoever. *The greater our innocence, the greater our strength and the swifter our victory.*"[23]

If the injustice is morally assimilable, then self-suffering can, and likely will, prick the conscience. But the potent brew of interest and ideology can easily persuade that those being rounded up harbor criminal intent and consequently deserve their fate. Did millions of innocent Jews being led to the crematoria "like lambs to the slaughter-house" prick the Nazi conscience? It might be said that they did not go smilingly and cheerfully—theirs was the "nonviolence of the weak"—but if the Nazis could morally rationalize the extermination of one million Jewish children—whose innocence of means and ends could be purer?—it is probable that they would also have rationalized the non-vindictive and voluntary self-immolation of the Jews.

To make sense of Gandhi's doctrine of *satyagraha* or, at any rate, to extract from it a rational core, a further distinction needs to be drawn between its differing "theaters" of action and protagonists. On some occasions, such as when a member in the intimacy of his ashram went astray, Gandhi pitched his fasts at, and they were designed to reform, the actual wrongdoer. Their efficacy hinged on the existence of moral and affective bonds between the wrongdoer and the fasting "penitent." The wrongdoer mends his or her ways because of both a genuine epiphany of having erred and solicitude for the beloved suffering penitent.[24]

On other occasions Gandhi pitched his fasts at, and they were designed to galvanize, a sympathetic public. The success of such self-suffering depended less on intimate bonds of affection, i.e., the "love" of Gandhi's person, than on a broad moral consensus, i.e., the manifest injustice of the situation that prompted his fast. In this instance, the venue is not private but public and concomitantly the target of the fast is not the wrongdoer but the bystander.

The confusion sets in when Gandhi conflates reforming a wrongdoer who is an intimate with reforming a bitter political opponent. Where mutual love binds the penitent and the wrongdoer, the former's self-suffering might very well sober up the latter. A Jewish mother's anguish has pulled many a wayward son back onto the straight and narrow. But it strains credulity that Gandhi's penance could, as he alleged, "melt" Hitler's heart.

Of course, the premise of Gandhi's doctrine is that feelings of love and a common humanity did bind Hitler and his victims. But even if he is right, and even if, on the remote chance, they could have been aroused from their slumber, is it at all plausible that these feelings would have stayed Hitler's demons? One would be hard-pressed to answer this question in the affirmative. The efficacy of penitential self-suffering to reform a wrongdoer diminishes the further removed the wrongdoer is. It might work with a wayward family member or friend, but not with an anonymous fellow citizen or some distant member of the human race. If the wrongdoer is also convinced that he is in the right and stands to materially lose if he is shown to be in the wrong, it is almost certain that self-suffering, however pure and intense, will leave him cold.

In short, it defies belief that, if the groups targeted by Hitler for extermination had practiced noncoercive, nonviolent resistance, they could have quickened his conscience and melted his heart. The only Gandhian strategies possibly effective against a Hitler would be noncooperation on a mass scale, and mobilizing sympathetic public opinion through self-suffering, in order, not to tug at his heartstrings, but to politically *defeat* him.

The exceptions to this rule are more apparent than real. True, Gandhi could direct a fast at a tyrannical British official whom he only knew from afar and in a formal capacity, yet the official proved responsive. If the official did relent, it was not, however, from a love of Gandhi, or because Gandhi's fast had fanned the embers of his conscience into life, but almost certainly because Gandhi's fast threatened to awaken the "dead conscience" of a sympathetic public and thereby politically isolate him.

A fast unto the death by Gandhi could also move anonymous millions of Hindus and Muslims to desist from intercommunal genocide. It was not, however, an emotional attachment per se to Gandhi that restrained them. Nor was it an awakened love of the "Other"—i.e., the mutual recognition by Hindus and Muslims of their common humanity—and self-knowledge that communal hatred was wrong.

If Indians ceased, momentarily, slaughtering each other, it was because of the mutual intuition that, when all was said and done, the Mahatma represented what was the highest and best in them, and had earned, through a lifetime of selfless devotion to public service, a claim on their obedience. It was a role that Gandhi had uniquely carved out for himself. Only a fast initiated by Gandhi, and him alone, could have cooled fratricidal hatreds whipped into a frenzy.

Self-suffering might move a loved one to mend his ways. It might also awaken the conscience of a public otherwise passive in the face of injustice. But as a rule it will not deter persons driven by righteous fury and defending perceived interests. Only a Gandhi could possess such overpowering spiritual force; it lived and died with his person. This was his great personal triumph, but also his great political failure. The tactic has no generalized value.

4/ PEOPLE'S MAN

What did *satyagraha* look like in action?

I will examine Gandhi's key political interventions during the period 1930–1947, when his ideas were put to their severest tests.

Discrimination and immorality. Gandhi launched his *satyagraha* campaigns to reform Indian society on the premise that a real or latent majority of Indians supported his social agenda. The point of each campaign was not to create a constituency ex nihilo, but through self-suffering to quicken the people's conscience on the basis of an already existing or incipient consensus. He aimed at "cultivating and ascertaining the opinion" of this preexisting constituency, and thus bring to bear the "force of public opinion" by awakening it from its slumber and "rous[ing]" it to a "sense of . . . duty."[1]

The target audience of Gandhi's campaigns was not the implacable opponents of reform but the actual or potential supporters of it, whom he wanted to goad into action. "The impending fast is against those who have faith in me," he declared on one such occasion.

Therefore, it is not against the English official world, but it is against those Englishmen and women who, in spite of the contrary teaching of the official world, believe in me and the justice of the cause I represent. Nor is it against those of my countrymen who have no faith in me, whether they be Hindus or others; but it is against those countless Indians . . . who believe that I represent a just cause. Above all, it is intended to sting the Hindu conscience into right religious action.[2]

And again: "What my penance should do is to quicken the conscience of those who know me and believe in my bona fides" and who "realized that [I] was their friend."[3]

Thus, in undertaking to remove the "blot" of untouchability by opening the doors of Hindu temples to the *Harijans* ("children of God"),[4] Gandhi presumed that a majority of Hindus supported such a reform: "the public is itself ready for it." The purpose of *satyagraha* was to coax the Hindu majority into acting on what it had already come to regard as right: "My opinion is that the mind of the majority is for this reform if it comes stealthily. Therefore, reformers should prepare the ground now ceaselessly and vigilantly to convert the passive attitude towards the reform into active approval thereof"; "The fast, if it has to come, will not be for the coercion of those who are opponents of the reform, but it will be intended to sting into action those who have been my comrades or who have taken pledges for the removal of untouchability. . . . My fast, therefore, ought not to affect the opponents of reform, nor even fellow-workers and the millions who have led me to believe that they were with me and the Congress in the campaign against untouchability, if the latter have on second thoughts come to the conclusion that untouchability is not after all a crime against God and humanity"; "The whole idea of my fast is based on the belief that a large section of the people favor temple-entry, but they do not voice it."[5]

In launching a campaign to rid India of the scourge of alcoholism, Gandhi likewise banked on the belief that "public opinion" could be consolidated around such a reform.[6] When challenged why he did not also wage campaigns to rid India of other debasing indulgences such as gambling, smoking and the cinema, Gandhi candidly responded: "The drink evil has been recognized as such by the people of this land. But the other evils are more or less fashionable"; "Smoking has attained alarming respectability. When a vice reaches that state, it becomes difficult to eradicate"; "These vices were fashionable and therefore were not capable of being dealt with like prohibition. I claim to be a practical reformer. I know almost instinctively what vices are ripe for being publicly dealt with."[7]

In other words, no amount of self-suffering would move the public to act against a vice that it did not already deplore. That being the case, Gandhi refused to squander precious time on deviancies of which the public did not already disapprove: "I would not discuss any matter which does not seem to be of immediate importance and about which there is the slightest room for doubt."[8]

To be sure, Gandhi did also profess that self-suffering would "finally break the wall of prejudice" of those violently opposed to his social reforms: "the hardest heart and the grossest ignorance," "the stoniest heart of the stoniest fanatic."[9] He also predicted that it would "melt the hearts" of those profiting from vice.[10] But still, the thrust of his campaigns was clearly to energize a latently sympathetic public via self-suffering, and utilize this "force of public opprobrium" in order to democratically overrule, or socially isolate, or force the capitulation of, or reach a principled compromise with, the diehards.[11]

Inequality and exploitation. Gandhi cast himself as the voice of India's impoverished "dumb millions": "I unhesitatingly say that I am a people's man. Every moment of my life I feel for the starving millions. I live and am prepared to lay down my life to relieve their sufferings and mitigate their miseries." When asked why he did not use a "thick mattress" and always traveled third class on the railway, Gandhi replied, "I do all I can to merge myself into the poor millions of India."[12]

Gandhi conceived *swaraj* as much more than political independence, or what he dismissively dubbed the "mere transfer of power." He sought the "complete deliverance of the toiling yet starving millions from the dreadful evil of economic serfdom" and "independence of the poorest and the lowliest in the land." "Unless poverty and unemployment are wiped out from India," he declared, "I would not agree that we have attained freedom."[13]

Beyond India's redemption Gandhi also aspired "to deliver the so-called weaker races of the earth from the crushing heels of Western exploitation in which England is the greatest partner." He expressed "hope" that the Indian struggle was "only part of the general struggle of colonial peoples against world capitalism and imperialism and that India is the vanguard in the world movement of colonial and agricultural masses for freedom, economic and political."[14]

By virtue of both his personal creed and India's crushing poverty, Gandhi adopted an austere code of what constituted just remuneration in a well-ordered society: "A thing not originally stolen must nevertheless be classified as stolen property if we possess it without needing it"; "whoever appropriates more than the minimum that is really necessary for him is guilty of theft"; "to live above the means befitting a poor country is to live on stolen food"; "each man shall have the wherewithal to supply all his natural needs and no more"; "The rich, moneyed man, who made his riches by exploitation or other questionable means, was no less guilty of robbery than the thief who picked a pocket or broke into a house and committed theft. Only the former took refuge behind the façade of respectability and escaped the penalty of law."[15]

To eradicate violence and crime, according to Gandhi, the "cruel inequality that obtains today"[16] must also be eliminated: "A nonviolent system of government is clearly an impossibility so long as the wide gulf between the rich and the hungry millions persists"; "No one has ever suggested that grinding pauperism can lead to anything else than moral degradation."[17]

Nonetheless Gandhi rejected the traditional demand of the Indian Left to forcibly expropriate large property-holders and nationalize the means of production. Instead he championed the "theory of trusteeship," according to which the owning class would be coaxed by nonviolent resistance to utilize its "excess" wealth for society's betterment: "I do not believe that the capitalists and landlords are all exploiters by an inherent necessity or that there is a basic or irreconcilable antagonism between their interests and those of the masses."[18]

Here is not the place to weigh the merits or demerits of Gandhi's trusteeship scheme.[19] I will also set aside the financial dependence of Gandhi on the Indian capitalists whom he shielded from popular wrath.[20] My concern is instead with the practicality of the means Gandhi proposed to realize his trusteeship goal.

Occasionally Gandhi foretold that the sacrifice and tenderness of their workers would convert property-owners from ruthless exploiters into enlightened guardians of the nation's patrimony. The rich would come to realize after "kind" gestures that they should not "squander [their] gains in luxurious or extravagant living, but must use them" for the poor: "I want, by means of suffering, to awaken them to their sense of duty, I want to melt their hearts and get them to render justice to their less fortunate brethren. They are human beings and my appeal to them will not go in vain"; "If we treat these rich people with decency, they would fulfill the expectations we have of them"; "If we win their confidence and put them at their ease, we will find that they are not averse to progressively sharing their riches with the masses"; "We should struggle against them in the same way and for the same reason, as lovingly and reluctantly and with as much respect and politeness as we do against our blood-relations."[21]

Just as Gandhi now and again suggested that the British would consent to India's independence if only their irrational fear and distrust were assuaged, so he suggested that the wealthy might cease exploiting the poor if only their "fear and distrust" could be assuaged.[22]

When pressed hard, however, Gandhi conceded that he could not point to a single precedent for his belief that self-suffering and love would convert greedy capitalists into philanthropic trustees, and that consequently his modus operandi amounted to a giant leap of faith.[23] Indeed, aren't capitalists convinced—and they don't lack in proofs of their own—that the system is fair, rewarding the enterprising few and penalizing the slothful many?

But Gandhi also exhorted the working class to organize and mobilize—that is, to realize its latent *power* and *coercive* force—if it wanted property-owners to distribute equitably their ill-gotten gains: "Immediately the worker realizes his strength, he is in a position to become a co-sharer with the capitalist instead of remaining his slave"; "What you must do is to demonstrate to the capitalists the power of labor and they will consent to be the trustees of those who toil for them"; "What is necessary is that laborers or workers should know their rights and should also know how to assert them"; "When the workers are better organized and more self-sacrificing, their power would grow. You are not conscious of your strength and therefore you are oppressed"; "As soon as laborers are properly educated and organized and they realize their strength, no amount of capital can subdue them. Organized and enlightened labor can dictate its own terms"; "[C]apitalists were after all few in number. The workers were many. But capital was well organized and had learnt to combine. If labor realized its inherent strength and the secret of combination it would rule capital instead of being ruled by it"; "There is in the English language a very potent word—all languages have it: 'No.' And the secret is that when capital wants labor to say 'Yes,' labor roars out 'No.' And immediately labor comes to recognize that it has the choice before it of saying 'No' when it wants to say 'No,' it has nothing to fear and it would not matter in the slightest degree that capital has guns and poison gas at its disposal. Capital will still be perfectly helpless if labor will assert its dignity making good its 'No.' Then labor does not need to retaliate, but stands defiant receiving the bullets and poison gas and still insists upon its 'No'"; "The peasant, whether as a landless laborer or a laboring proprietor, comes first. He is the son of the soil which rightly belongs or should belong to him, not to the absentee landlord. . . . He has so to work as to make it impossible for the landlord to exploit him. Closest cooperation amongst the peasants is absolutely necessary."[24]

If moral appeals did not persuade Indian industrialists and landlords to "become guardians of the poor in the true sense of the term and the latter are more and more crushed and die of hunger," then Gandhi advocated "nonviolent noncooperation and civil disobedience as the right and infallible means."[25] Indeed, he warned the haves that unless they gave up their ill-gotten gains anarchy would ensue: "There is no other choice than between voluntary surrender on the part of the capitalist of superfluities and consequent acquisition of the real happiness of all, on the one hand, and on the other, the impending chaos into which, if the capitalist does not wake up betimes, awakened but ignorant, famishing millions will plunge the country and which not even the armed force that a powerful Government can bring into play can avert."[26]

Still, Gandhi formally abjured "so-called class-conflict,"[27] counseling instead that "landlords and capitalists" be "persuaded and converted,"[28] and often expressed disdain for worker strikes.[29] He could be willfully blind to the glaring fact that his practical prescription for abolishing exploitation and inequality ultimately relied not on the beneficence of self-suffering but on the coercion of raw (if nonviolent) power.[30]

Aggression and occupation. In the course of World War II, Gandhi conjured up sometimes complementary, sometimes contradictory scenarios to defeat Axis aggression nonviolently. It appeared as if he were desperately straining and improvising to prove the viability and relevance of *satyagraha* in the face of its ultimate challenge.

Noncooperation. Once the Axis powers realized that they could not exploit conquered territories without the occupied population's cooperation, Gandhi speculated, they would withdraw: in the face of "quiet, dignified and nonviolent defiance," the "tyrant will not find it worth his while to go on with his terrorism," and "he would certainly have been obliged to retire." Whatever Gandhi formally preached, this tactic plainly made appeal not to the consciences or hearts of the conquerors but to their balance-sheets, i.e., material self-interest.[31] In a variation of this scenario Gandhi concluded that noncooperation would not result in mass slaughter because Hitler did not want to exploit the British Empire but rather he sought to vanquish it—to get it to "admit defeat"—and, consequently, if denied the adrenaline stimulus of a hunt, "he will lack the zest to kill you. Every hunter has had this experience. No one has ever heard of anyone hunting cows."[32]

If the conquering power did not withdraw and committed atrocities, Gandhi conjectured in the war's early stages, the number of persons killed would still be fewer if the captive population practiced nonviolent resistance, while Europe as a whole would emerge from the bloodbath spiritually redeemed:

> Imagine the state of Europe today if the Czechs, the Poles, the Norwegians, the French and the English had all said to Hitler: "You need not make your scientific preparation for destruction. We will meet

your violence with nonviolence. You will therefore be able to destroy our nonviolent army without tanks, battleships and airships." It may be retorted that the only difference would be that Hitler would have got without fighting what he has gained after a bloody fight. Exactly. The history of Europe would then have been written differently. Possession might (but only might) have been then taken under non-violent resistance, as it has been taken now after per-petration of untold barbarities. Under nonviolence only those would have been killed who had trained themselves to be killed, if need be, without killing anyone and without bearing malice towards any-body. I daresay that in that case Europe would have added several inches to its moral stature. And in the end I expect it is the moral worth that will count. All else is dross.[33]

But if the conquering power did wipe out the nonco-operating captive population, such an outcome, according to Gandhi, would still be preferable to violent resistance. Thus, "the Czechs may be annihilated for disobedience to orders," but "that would be a glorious victory for the Czechs." They would still have preserved intact their "soul, i.e., honor." It would also spell "the beginning of the fall of Germany" because—or so Gandhi believed—aggres-sors might be able to massacre innocents one time but "an army that dares to pass over corpses would not be able to repeat that experience."[34] He likewise counseled his own compatriots, "if the Führer attacked India" and even if he mercilessly slaughtered Indians refusing to cooperate, still, "these *satyagrahis* facing the army will go down in history as heroes and heroines at least equal to those of whom we learn in fables or cold history."[35]

Self-suffering. But what if the conquering power sought not the cooperation but instead the displacement and dispossession of the captive population, or its outright extermination? Keeping his faith in the efficacy of self-suffering and an upwelling of love, Gandhi professed that nonviolent resistance could deter a mad and murderous despot because "human nature in its essence is one and therefore unfailingly responds to the advances of love."[36]

In the face of skeptics and naysayers Gandhi stubbornly rejoined:

> *As a believer in nonviolence, I am not limiting its possibilities. Hitherto [Hitler] and his likes have built upon their invariable experience that men yield to force. Unarmed men, women and children offering nonviolent resistance without any bitterness in them will be a novel experience for them. Who can dare say it is not in their nature to respond to the higher and finer forces? They have the same soul as I have.*

> *If the Jews . . . adopt active nonviolence, i.e., fellow-feeling for the gentile Germans deliberately, they cannot do any harm to the Germans and I am as certain as I am dictating these lines that the stoniest German heart will melt.*

> *Sufferings of the nonviolent have been known to melt the stoniest hearts. I make bold to say that if the Jews can summon to their aid the soul power that comes only from nonviolence, Herr Hitler will bow before the courage which he has never yet experienced.*

I do not despair of [Hitler] responding to human suffering even though caused by him. But I must refuse to believe that the Germans as a nation have no heart or markedly less than the other nations of the earth.

[The Axis powers] belong to the same species as the so-called democracies or, better still, war-resisters themselves. They show in their family circles the same tenderness, affection, consideration and generosity that war-resisters are likely to show even outside such circles. The difference is only of degree. . . . It is therefore a matter of rule of three to find out the exact amount of nonviolence required to melt the harder hearts of the Fascists and the Nazis, if it is assumed, as it is, the so-called democracies melt before a given amount of nonviolence.

Even a Nero is not devoid of a heart. The unexpected spectacle of endless rows upon rows of men and women simply dying rather than surrender to the will of an aggressor must ultimately melt him away and his soldiery.

Indeed it is not quite inconceivable that the loving sacrifice of many may bring an insane man to his senses. Instances are not wanting of absolutely insane people having come back to their senses.

Nonviolent action, if it is adequate, must influence Hitler and easily the duped Germans. No man can be turned into a permanent machine.

I must adhere to my faith in the possibility of the most debased human nature to respond to nonviolence. . . . I will not belittle the power of nonviolence or distrust the Führer's capacity to respond to true nonviolence.

Some people say that satyagraha *is of no avail against a person who has no moral sense. I join issue with that. The stoniest heart must melt if we are true and have patience. I have met human monsters from my early youth. I have found that even they are not beyond redemption if we know how to touch the right chord in their soul.*[37]

It is hard not to respect the resilience of Gandhi's faith. But it is also hard not to see the obvious flaws in it. If Hitler was genuinely persuaded of the necessity of lebensraum (living space) and the malignity of the Jews, and if expanding Germany's borders and eliminating Jews and other "defective" people served Germany's interests (as he construed them), why should suffering allied to love have converted him?

In fact, just as Gandhi conceded that noncooperation in the face of the Axis invaders might result in mass, albeit redemptive, death, so he was less than totally convinced of the efficacy of self-suffering, at any rate in the here and now. Thus he also advised that, if the Nazis proved implacable foes, Jews should go mutely to their deaths because such a dignified sacrifice would be their ultimate salvation: "If the Jewish mind could be prepared for voluntary suffering, even the massacre [of Jews by Hitler] . . . could be turned into a day of thanksgiving and joy that Jehovah had wrought deliverance of the race even at the hands of the tyrant. For the God-fearing, death has no terror. It is a joyful sleep to be followed by a waking that would be all the more refreshing for the long sleep." And again: "It is highly probable that, as the writer says, 'a Jewish Gandhi in Germany, should one arise, could function for about five minutes and would be promptly taken to the guillotine.' But that will not disprove my case or shake my belief in the efficacy of *ahimsa*. I can conceive the necessity of the immolation of hundreds, if not thousands, to appease the hunger of dictators who have not believed in *ahimsa*. . . . Sufferers need not see the result during their lifetime. They must have faith that if their cult survives, the result is a certainty."[38]

GANDHI AND THE NAZI HOLOCAUST

Gandhi has been harshly criticized for counseling martyrdom to European Jewry during the Nazi holocaust. But he also repeatedly and with uncharacteristic fervor denounced the murderous Nazi assault. "The German persecution of the Jews," he declared, "seems to have no parallel in history. The tyrants of old never went so mad as Hitler seems to have gone. . . . If there ever could be a justifiable war in the name of and for humanity, a war against Germany, to prevent the wanton persecution of a whole race, would be completely justified."[39]

Gandhi also retrospectively advised willful self-immolation to the Japanese victims of the atomic bomb. They should have "come out in the open and let the pilot see that [they] have not a trace of ill-will against him. . . . If those thousands who were done to death in Hiroshima . . . had died with that prayerful action—died openly with that prayer in their hearts—their sacrifice would not have gone in vain."[40] And, as already shown, Gandhi recommended martyrdom to the Czech nation and other actual and potential victims of Axis aggression.

During the fratricidal bloodletting at the time of India's partition, Gandhi proclaimed, "I do not mind if each and every one of the 500 [Hindu] families in your area [of East Bengal] is done to death [by Muslims]," and "if all the [Hindu] Punjabis were to die to the last man without killing, the Punjab would become immortal." He also willed the death of all Kashmiris, *including the children*—"everybody, young and old, should die there valiantly"—to prevent the province's dismemberment by foreign marauders.[41]

In short, Gandhi's pronouncements on the Nazi holocaust might have been callous, but they also had the merit, albeit a dubious one, of consistency.

If the goal of *satyagraha* was to melt Hitler's heart in the promise of *earthly* deliverance, yet it produces no results during the terrestrial life of the sufferers, then it must be reckoned a *political* failure. Put otherwise, if all Gandhi had to offer his disciples was posthumous redemption, it is unlikely that the political movement he led would have had broad reach. The expectation of earthly reward was implicit in his political message. Otherwise, why did he call himself a "*practical* reformer" and a "*practical* idealist"?

It is of course the nature of politics to carry in it a high probability of defeat, and a meaningful political victory almost always comes after many setbacks and lives lost. But it goes against the grain of the political vocation to counsel a tactic that, however exalting, has no prospect of success in the here and now—and melting Hitler's heart through self-suffering would appear to fall squarely in the "no prospect" column. Of course, it might be argued that, whatever European Jewry did, its fate was sealed and, in the face of certain death, nonviolent resistance would have been the most redemptive form of martyrdom.[42] That, however, is a matter altogether separate and apart from the question of whether self-suffering is a viable tactic against a fanatical enemy. The answer to this question must be an emphatic, if regrettable, "no."

What held for Hitler also held for Gandhi's nemesis in the epic struggle for Indian independence. Winston Churchill was hardly persuaded by Indian suffering to dismantle the British Empire.[43] The interest-cum-ideology of Westminster easily trumped the suffering-cum-love of the Indian downtrodden.

Gandhi himself harbored few illusions about what dictated official British policy: "It is the material benefits which England derives from the connection [with India] that matter to the British public. It is the extinction of those benefits that matters most to the Indian masses who can no longer bear the crushing burden"; "The Government, instead of telling us, show by their many unmistakable acts that they will do anything but sacrifice the material interest of their principals, the British manufacturers and the like, who live on India's exploitation"; "The British troops are in India not to protect India but to protect British interests which were imposed on India and which are now so well entrenched that even the British Government cannot dislodge them. The British did not come here as philanthropists, nor is there any altruism in their continued stay here."[44]

"The English Ministers are pursuing what they believe to be an honest policy," Gandhi further noted. "It is their honest belief that British rule in India has been, on the whole, for her good. They honestly believe that under it India has advanced."[45]

If British policy was dictated by material interest; and if the British "will do anything but sacrifice the material interest"; and if ideology effectively rationalized this self-interested policy, making it appear not just benign but beneficial to Indians: then, should it surprise that—contrary to Gandhi's starry-eyed expectations—the martyrdom of Indians failed to touch British imperialists, or that it failed to get "British commerce with India . . . purified of greed" and thereby put on "terms of mutual help and . . . equally suited to both"?[46]

Although Gandhi spoke of wanting to "convert the administrators of the system," he nonetheless qualified, "the conversion may or may not be willing."[47] And again: "to convert them or, if you will, even to drive them out of the country."[48] By the same token, although Gandhi spoke of wanting to "wake up public conscience as also that of the authority," he nonetheless qualified, "assuming that the latter can have any conscience at all."[49] These caveats suggest that Gandhi intended to rely on more than love-power to wrest independence from Great Britain.

In fact Gandhi conceived the struggle against British imperialism in terms of making India ungovernable, and consequently unprofitable. His modus operandi combined nonviolence, which neutralized British bayonets by making British resort to them politically untenable; economic boycott, which targeted British exports to India; and non-cooperation, which nullified British authority by flouting it.

Thus, far from trying to melt the hearts of British official-dom, he foretold and forewarned: "In case India's demand [for independence] is not granted, there is bound to be a fierce boycott, and all the attention of Great Britain will have to be absorbed in looking after her quickly-perishing trade interests in India"; "If, notwithstanding their desire to the contrary, they saw that their guns and everything they had created for the consolidation of their authority were useless because of our non-use of them, they could not do otherwise than bow to the inevitable and either retire from the scene, or remain on our terms, i.e., as friends to cooperate with us, not as rulers to impose their will upon us"; "Whether we convert them or not, we are determined to make their rule impossible by nonviolent noncooperation."[50]

On many an occasion Gandhi repudiated the use of force to attain independence: "It is my confirmed belief that if India adheres to the path of peace till the very end, the hearts of the most callous British officers are bound to undergo a change"; "By self-suffering I seek to convert [the Englishman], never to destroy him." But truth be told, he did not seek to spiritually convert the wrong-doing British imperialists. Instead, he set out to coerce them, albeit non-violently, into submission.

Gandhi endeavored to harness the latent power of the Indian people in a tit-for-tat confrontation with the British Empire. His actual means, as he admitted in moments of candor, had to be "force of will" and "matching forces," because "the chief obstacle in the way of *swaraj*" was "the unwillingness of the British officials to part with power."[51] And again: "This much is certain, that argument is not what will carry conviction. The British conviction will be in exact proportion to the strength we have developed." And yet again: "How can this British mentality be changed or, in other words, how can power be wrested from such unwilling hands? No argument will carry conviction to these statesmen; they are all seasoned hard-headed soldiers. They like and appreciate facts, deeds. *They will understand an open rebellion.*"[52]

But Gandhi also held out the hope of reaching the British "nation," i.e., "public opinion," through self-suffering: "I have deliberately used the word 'conversion.' For my ambition is no less than to convert the British people through nonviolence, and thus make them see the wrong they have done to India."[53] The British imperialists might have to be driven out, but the conscience of the British *people* might yet be pricked. Indeed, British public opinion could serve as a critical weapon for coercing dyed-in-the-wool British imperialists to leave India.

Additionally, Gandhi counted on the international community to stay the hand of British imperialism. "The British Government, powerful though it is," he observed during the Salt March, "is sensitive to world opinion which will not tolerate repression of extreme political agitation which civil disobedience undoubtedly is, so long as disobedience remains civil and, therefore, necessarily nonviolent."[54]

In his final reckoning Gandhi acknowledged that, if the British finally decided to pack up and leave, it was not because Indians had tugged at their heartstrings but because they had upended the exchequer's balance-sheet: "The British are bound to quit this country. They are a nation of businessmen. They calculate the profit and loss from every transaction. They have realized that it is no longer profitable to rule India"; "I know the English better than anyone else. They are leaving India because they know that they can derive no economic gain from continuing their rule in India and they have realized that politically they can no longer keep us in subjection."[55]

It was not the power of love but the juggernaut of power that cleared the path to India's independence.

CONCLUSION

A wave of popular revolts is now sweeping the planet.

In many instances, it was an act of nonviolent civil resistance that either sparked the local uprising or marked its turning-point.

In Tunisia, it was the self-immolation of a street vendor. In Cairo, it was the assault by goons on camelback against nonviolent protesters in Tahrir Square. In New York City, it was the voluntary mass arrest of demonstrators on the Brooklyn Bridge.

These actions "quickened" the public conscience. People who had stood by indifferently and passively for decades suddenly came to life.

The acts of nonviolent resistance resonated with a broad public because of an already existing consensus that the system was unjust.

In spirit and form, the epic events of the past year appear like a page out of Gandhi's life.

But it is also easy to see the limitations of Gandhi's teachings.

Neither Ben-Ali of Tunisia nor Mubarak of Egypt was "melted" by the people's self-suffering. They had to be *forced* from power. Neither the liberal mayor of Oakland nor the liberal mayor of New York let their bleeding hearts prevent them from brutally clearing out the "Occupy" movement.

Self-suffering might sting the conscience of the 99 percent and get them to act. But only the concerted and courageous power of the overwhelming majority will get the 1 percent to budge and be gone.

The only language that the 1 percent understand, as Gandhi conceded in his more candid moments, is "open rebellion."

Still, Gandhi had a point. However costly the price in lives of nonviolent resistance, it is probably still less than the price of violent rebellion, while a nonviolent struggle augurs better for the future than an armed struggle.

Once armed foreign forces entered Libya in "support" of the popular revolt, the number of deaths skyrocketed. The probable order of magnitude is manyfold greater than the total deaths in any of the other revolts convulsing the Arab world. The result of the armed victory in Libya is a power once again in thrall to external forces and likely to make most Libyans soon yearn for a return to the days of Qaddafi.[1]

"Violence may destroy one or more bad rulers, but," Gandhi warned, "others will pop up in their places."

The unspoken prejudice against nonviolence is that it is cowardly and unmanly. But nonviolence as Gandhi conceived it can hardly be dismissed on these counts. It takes an awful lot of bravery to march unarmed into the line of fire "smilingly" and "cheerfully," and get oneself blown to pieces.

In his last days and amidst inter-communal slaughter, Gandhi insisted on opening his prayer services in Hindu temples with a verse from the Koran. It enraged Hindu fanatics to the point that one of them finally murdered him.

Who would be so bold as to deny that Gandhi's was a heroic death?

If a criticism is to be leveled against Gandhi's nonviolence, it is that he sets the bar of courage too high for most mortals to vault.

It is a central conceit of Gandhi's doctrine that nonviolent resistance in the face of evil is not only more ethical than violence but could also achieve the same results.

The jury is still out on this.

It is certainly doubtful, as Arundhati Roy has pointed out, that nonviolent resistance can achieve *any* results against a ferocious enemy acting outside the glare of public scrutiny.

But what can be said with confidence is that the results of violent resistance have been at best mixed.

The day after, bloody revolutions seem always to disappoint, and in the scramble to the top, those with the most blood on their hands seem always to get there first.

The challenge for the younger generation as it embarks on the struggle to remake the world is to see how far it can advance without having to use violence.

The further along it gets nonviolently, the more likely it is that the new world will also be a better one.

NOTES

CHAPTER ONE

1. For the origin and meaning of the term *satyagraha*, see Stanley Wolpert, *Gandhi's Passion: The life and legacy of Mahatma Gandhi* (Oxford: 2001), p. 66.

2. I will be citing from *The Collected Works of Mahatma Gandhi* published by the Ministry of Information and Broadcasting, Government of India. Hereafter: **CW**.

3. I will be citing from Mahatma Gandhi, *The Essential Writings*, edited with an introduction and notes by Judith M. Brown (Oxford: 2008). Hereafter: **EW**. I will also be citing from M. K. Gandhi, *Non-violent Resistance (Satyagraha)* (Mineola, NY: 2001). Hereafter: **NR**.

4. CW, v. 70, p. 203. In the opinion of famed French novelist Romain Rolland, who was also Gandhi's biographer, however: "His mind proceeds through successive experiments into action and he follows a straight line, but he never stops, and one would risk error in attempting to judge him by what he said ten years ago, because his thought is in constant evolution" (CW, v. 48, p. 499).

5. CW, v. 69, pp. 291-92, CW, v. 73, pp. 276-77.

6. CW, v. 71, pp. 315-16, CW, v. 80, p. 222, CW, v. 82, p. 162.

7. I will be citing from M. K. Gandhi, *Hind Swaraj and Other Writings*, edited by Anthony J. Parel (Cambridge: 1997). Hereafter: **HS**.

8. CW, v. 42, p. 125, CW, v. 45, pp. 332-33, CW, v. 70, p. 242, CW, v. 80, p. 325, CW, v. 81, p. 319, CW, v. 82, p. 350.

9. CW, v. 67, p. 284.

10. CW, v. 42, p. 469, CW, v. 43, p. 307, CW, v. 46, p. 6 ("Charges," "apparent"), CW, v. 47, p. 378. In his most lucid, candid and, as it were, consistent statement, Gandhi wrote:

> An apparent inconsistency either in my life or in the affairs of the Ashram can be explained. There is only an appearance of inconsistency in the action of a person who wraps up his body in winter and keeps it uncovered in summer. He obeys the same principle both when he covers the body and when he leaves it uncovered. Many such seeming inconsistencies can be properly explained. Other inconsistencies are such in fact. They are due to my or [the] Ashram's weaknesses. They should be regarded as moral deficiencies and every effort should be made to overcome them. Which inconsistencies are really such and which are only apparent ones can be decided only when we examine all of them one by one. (CW, v. 49, pp. 66-67)

11. CW, v. 66, p. 438 ("deviate"), CW, v. 74, p. 330 ("entirety"), CW, v. 78, p. 37 ("pure"), CW, v. 86, p. 315.

12. Gandhi tried convincing British authorities during the Zulu War to arm his Indian volunteers but they refused.

13. On the last point, see Wolpert, *Gandhi's Passion*, p. 97.

14. CW, v. 66, p. 438 ("army"), CW, v. 67, p. 285.

15. CW, v. 89, pp. 432-33.

16. CW, v. 42, p. 437, CW, v. 68, p. 269, NR, p. 132; but see also Wolpert, *Gandhi's Passion*, p. 137.

17. CW, v. 63, pp. 373-74, CW, v. 72, pp. 30-31.

18. "Wybergh to Gandhi," 3 May 1910, reproduced in HS, pp. 139-40.

19. CW, v. 45, pp. 365-66.

20. HS, pp. 62-65.

21. CW, v. 44, p. 7.

22. CW, v. 55, p. 411 ("examination"), CW, v. 89, p. 295 ("prompting"). Here, the contradiction is perhaps less acute than meets the eye: insofar as, according to Gandhi, "God alone knows the intentions" (CW, v. 72, p. 433, CW, v. 89, p. 295), in effect a man could only be judged by his action.

In still another permutation Gandhi asserted that "if the motive and the action are pure, the doer is not responsible for the manifold consequences that may arise from it" (CW, v. 45, p. 230).

23. CW, v. 53, p. 216, CW, v. 54, p. 416, CW, v. 67, p. 284 ("pickets"), CW, v. 68, pp. 457-59.

24. CW, v. 71, p. 205.

25. CW, v. 68, pp. 81-82 ("classical"), CW, v. 86, pp. 397-98.

26. CW, v. 71, p. 225 ("world"), CW, v. 75, p. 339.

27. CW, v. 70, pp. 204 ("sympathies"), 237, CW, v. 75, p. 272, CW, v. 76, pp. 400-1 ("difference," "resolving"), CW, v. 80, p. 294 ("creed"). Gandhi also supported the Allies because allegedly they were victims of Axis aggression fighting defensive wars (CW, v. 71, pp. 10-11, CW, v. 72, p. 377).

28. CW, v. 69, p. 122, CW, v. 72, p. 60, CW, v. 73, pp. 72, 85, 254, CW, v. 74, pp. 17, 27 ("enslaving"), 115, CW, v. 75, pp. 10 ("Churchillism"), 37, 45, 72, 205, CW, v. 84, p. 394. In an especially harsh statement bracketing the Allies with the Axis, Gandhi wrote:

> What is a war criminal? Was not war itself a crime against God and humanity and, therefore, were not all those who sanctioned, engineered, and conducted wars, war criminals? War criminals are not confined to the Axis Powers alone. Roosevelt and Churchill are no less war criminals than Hitler and Mussolini. Hitler was "Great Britain's sin." Hitler is only an answer to British imperialism, and this I say in spite of the fact that I hate Hitlerism and its anti-Semitism. England, America and Russia have all of them got their hands dyed more or less red—not merely Germany and Japan. The Japanese have only proved themselves to be apt pupils of the West. They have learnt at the feet of the West and beaten it at its own game. (CW, v. 79, pp. 422-23)

29. CW, v. 59, p. 45 ("evil"), CW, v. 72, p. 187 ("mockery").

30. CW, v. 68, pp. 137-41, 205, CW, v. 69, p. 290, CW, v. 72, p. 230. I return to this point below.

31. CW, v. 70, p. 224, CW, v. 73, p. 208 ("essentially"), CW, v. 79, p. 424 ("logic"), CW, v. 83, p. 180 ("academic"), CW, v. 86, p. 200 ("idealist"). Gandhi consciously pitched his

language, notable for its simplicity and accessibility, "with the general public in view, and not . . . men of learning" (CW, v. 45, p. 2).

32. He was also more likely to capitulate to an interlocutor if faced with a moral plea rather than a reasoned argument; attached limited value to reason in and of itself as a persuasive force; and believed that "reason, as a rule, follows in the footsteps of feeling" (CW, v. 45, p. 244, CW, v. 48, p. 369, CW, v. 90, p. 216).

33. CW, v. 78, p. 16.

34. CW, v. 47, p. 253, CW, v. 79, p. 424 ("sacrifice"), CW, v. 85, p. 368.

35. CW, v. 49, pp. 80-81; but cf. CW, v. 44, p. 357, where he enters the qualification: "We cannot always live up to an ideal and sometimes in actual practice we have to compromise it in order that we may not be forced to give it up altogether."

36. CW, v. 71, p. 257. But he could also be cautious in his political judgments, as when he replied to a query on Bolshevik rule in Russia, "It is perhaps somewhat shameful that I have to confess to you that I do not yet know exactly what Bolshevism is for the simple reason that I have not had time to study the inner working of the Russian revolution" (CW, v. 46, p. 295). Later, while imprisoned during World War II, Gandhi read extensively on socialist and communist doctrine, including Marx's *Capital* (CW, v. 78, p. 69, CW, v. 82, p. 335). He was much better read than he generally let on. The image he projected of an intellectual simpleton, however ingenuous, should be taken with a grain of salt. For the breadth and depth of his reading, see CW, v. 49, pp. 76-77, CW, v. 50, p. 310; but cf. CW, v. 50, pp. 361-62, for Gandhi's confessed ignorance of some of the Western classics.

37. CW, v. 45, p. 7; cf. CW, v. 88, p. 17, where he expresses disdain for "cinemas and theaters," although he had been to "the theater only once, when I was a small child," and CW, v. 90, p. 340, where he counsels that in newly independent India "there should be no place for cinema."

38. CW, v. 43, pp. 336-38, CW, v. 74, pp. 114-16, 132, CW, v. 83, p. 333.

39. CW, v. 44, p. 18.

40. CW, v. 43, p. 321 ("heart"), CW, v. 47, p. 399, CW, v. 73, p. 407 ("sustains"), CW, v. 81, p. 244 ("question"), CW, v. 82, p. 368, CW, v. 83, p. 258 ("root"); but cf. CW, v. 86, p. 338.

41. CW, v. 48, p. 412 ("real"), CW, v. 69, pp. 226-27; but cf. CW, v. 78, p. 8, CW, v. 79, p. 39, CW, v. 80, p. 238, CW, v. 86, p. 429, where Gandhi allows, "You may call yourself an atheist, but so long as you feel akin with mankind you accept God in practice," and also contradictorily states regarding communists, "I dislike the idea of excluding anybody because of his label," and "I have no difficulty in working side by side with communists."

42. CW, v. 42, p. 422, CW, v. 43, p. 32, CW, v. 45, p. 213 ("guided"), CW, v. 47, p. 292, CW, v. 49, p. 482 ("depend"), CW, v. 51, pp. 70, 114, 222, 341, CW, v. 71, p. 306, CW, v. 73, pp. 91, 156, CW, v. 78, pp. 259, 293. But cf. CW, v. 43, p. 32, CW, v. 74, p. 279, CW, v. 85, p. 17, where Gandhi somewhat qualifies, "It has been my experience, with regard to myself and many others, that after one has heard the inner voice, one finds arguments in support of it"; "Many of my activities are undertaken in good faith or intuitively. But they are not conducted on the basis of inspiration alone; I have tried to place my convictions on a sound scientific foundation while propagating them"; "I myself have not followed my instinct unless my reason backed it . . . before the fast began, my reason was able to back up my instinct." It should further be noted that he was not oblivious to political realities on the ground when faith summoned him to act; rather the contrary (CW, v. 71, p. 338). For the meaning Gandhi attached to his "inner voice," cf. CW, v. 50, p. 326.

43. CW, v. 51, p. 64.

44. CW, v. 74, p. 2; but cf. CW, v. 83, p. 180, and NR, p. 109, where Gandhi makes modest claims for *satyagraha* as a "science." The "laws" he derived from his science were no less murky— e.g., "the law of civil resistance [is that] it is never needed to be applied perpetually to a cause. Its sovereign efficacy lies in the fact that it secures redress within a measurable though previously unascertainable period" (CW, v. 47, p. 252). Incidentally, Gandhi contradicted this "law" of civil resistance during World War II when he conceded that it might not be efficacious against the Nazis and the *satyagrahis*

would *en masse* have to accept martyrdom without earthly redemption (see below).

45. CW, v. 42, p. 423, CW, v. 61, p. 113, CW, v. 72, p. 230, CW, v. 86, pp. 155, 183, 262-63, 368, CW, v. 89, p. 121 ("votary"), NR, pp. 286-87; but cf. CW, v. 73, p. 175.

46. CW, v. 72, p. 307; see CW, v. 62, p. 29, for his "five simple axioms of nonviolence," and CW, v. 63, p. 262, for his enumeration "without argument" of the "implications and conditions of success of nonviolence."

47. CW, v. 45, p. 127 ("independent," "essence"), CW, v. 49, p. 38 ("certainly"), CW, v. 80, p. 306 ("everybody"), CW, v. 88, p. 160 ("blindly").

48. CW, v. 71, pp. 103-4 ("authority," "experienced"), CW, v. 73, p. 31 ("author").

49. CW, v. 47, p. 372 ("within"), CW, v. 73, p. 53 ("confident").

50. CW, v. 48, p. 156 ("superficial," "books"), CW, v. 88, p. 1; but cf. CW, v. 53, p. 216, CW, v. 88, p. 325, where Gandhi avows, "I claim no monopoly of the knowledge of the doctrine of *satyagraha*, it is open to anyone to give what meaning he likes to *satyagraha* and lay down rules also according to his liking"; "It is not, however, claimed that all the laws of *satyagraha* have already been formulated. I cannot say either that I myself know all the laws."

51. CW, v. 78, p. 69.

52. CW, v. 43, p. 381, CW, v. 44, p. 47, CW, v. 51, pp. 53, 64, CW, v. 81, p. 212 ("rule"), CW, v. 82, pp. 141-42 ("restrictions"), CW, v. 83, p. 401 ("embarking"), CW, v. 88, p. 168 ("*shastra*"), CW, v. 90, pp. 377, 461.

53. CW, v. 78, p. 234.

54. CW, v. 71, p. 258 ("destroyed"), CW, v. 79, pp. 187, 382, CW, v. 89, p. 396.

55. CW, v. 44, p. 170 (pencil), CW, v. 49, pp. 167 (conversing), 200 (conversing), CW, v. 73, p. 444 ("jokes," "pleasantries"), CW, v. 79, pp. 68 (wristwatches), 292 (underwear), CW, v. 81, p. 192 (pencil), CW, v. 90, p. 354 (he favored a reed pen).

56. A bit of the Big Brother also lurked in Gandhi. He agreed that members of his ashram should keep "a personal diary of their work, thoughts and ideas . . ., and place them before [him] for his perusal so that he could know the mind and work of each

and every Ashramite, and make necessary suggestions" (CW, v. 42, pp. 283-84, CW, v. 73, p. 416n1, CW, v. 74, pp. 291-92, CW, v. 79, p. 380).

57. CW, v. 43, p. 32, CW, v. 45, p. 135, CW, v. 66, p. 105, CW, v. 68, p. 59 ("handful"), CW, v. 72, pp. 378-81, 450, CW, v. 73, pp. 388, 427, CW, v. 75, pp. 137, 146-66, CW, v. 78, pp. 64, 78, 218-19, CW, v. 81, pp. 87-89, EW, p. 15. For the meaning Gandhi attached to *purna swaraj*, and the distinction he made out between it and "independence," cf. CW, v. 45, pp. 263-64.

58. CW, v. 67, p. 123.

CHAPTER TWO

1. CW, v. 67, p. 437 ("thought"), CW, v. 68, p. 45 ("incapable"). For Gandhi's expansive notion of nonviolence as well as the practical exceptions he makes for it, see CW, v. 50, pp. 205-8.

2. CW, v. 68, pp. 29 ("universe"), 189 ("unadulterated"), CW, v. 69, p. 70 ("goodness"). Gandhi did not extend the ambit of his doctrine of nonviolence to include "sub-human species," on the pragmatic grounds that his was not a religious program but a political one designed to convert a broad constituency, although he himself "would not kill insects, scorpions or even snakes. Nor should I under any circumstances take meat" (CW, v. 61, p. 95, CW, v. 72, pp. 454-55, CW, v. 73, p. 385).

3. HS, p. 90.

4. CW, v. 48, p. 224 ("persists"), CW, v. 50, p. 207, CW, v. 71, p. 408 ("extinct"), CW, v. 90, p. 195 ("destructive").

5. CW, v. 67, pp. 436-37 ("clans," "humankind," "family"), EW, pp. 324-26, NR, p. 179.

6. CW, v. 68, pp. 46 ("hell"), 204.

7. CW, v. 73, pp. 253-55. The British suppressed publication of what Gandhi continued to believe was a "good letter" (CW, v. 73, p. 288).

8. CW, v. 69, p. 69, CW, v. 72, p. 456, CW, v. 75, p. 60, CW, v. 78, p. 225, EW, p. 335, NR, pp. 32, 72, 149. Gandhi seemed however to consider the "shaming" of a wrongdoer legitimate (EW, pp. 206, 336, CW, v. 83, p. 268).

9. CW, v. 71, p. 403, NR, pp. 182, 185-86.

10. CW, v. 69, p. 73 ("potent"), HS, p. 146.

11. CW, v. 69, p. 69.

12. CW, v. 43, pp. 93, 338.

13. CW, v. 43, p. 339.

14. CW, v. 71, p. 225.

15. CW, v. 66, p. 421, EW, p. 56 ("distinguishes").

16. CW, v. 43, p. 133, CW, v. 45, p. 360, CW, v. 59, p. 42 ("pop"), CW, v. 72, pp. 136, 217 ("blind"), HS, pp. 77-78 (esp. footnotes 151, 152), 81 ("seed").

17. CW, v. 45, p. 249.

18. CW, v. 45, p. 349.

19. CW, v. 46, pp. 1-3, 29-31, CW, v. 48, p. 338 ("worst").

20. CW, v. 72, pp. 214 ("deliverance"), 229, CW, v. 73, pp. 26-27 ("superior"), 324, CW, v. 75, p. 441 ("stronger").

21. CW, v. 72, p. 214. Towards the end of World War II Gandhi seemed to qualify this prognostication with the caveat that only if India were not freed would the Allies' victory inevitably wreak future horrors (CW, v. 79, pp. 131-32).

22. CW, v. 86, pp. 116 ("out-Hitlering"), 247-48 ("super-Hitlerism"), 436 ("crushed").

23. CW, v. 75, p. 441. For a variation of this argument in the instance of a rapist's assault, see CW, v. 68, pp. 81-82.

24. CW, v. 72, p. 229.

25. I will only consider here Gandhi's differentiated approach to violence against other human beings. For Gandhi's dissent from the sanctity Jainism attaches to all nonhuman life, because "in life it is impossible to eschew violence completely," cf. CW, v. 84, pp. 230-32, 391-92.

26. CW, v. 51, pp. 18-19, 24-25 (in this last passage Gandhi enters the additional caveat that for such resistance to be truly nonviolent, "One's aim should not be to inflict pain nor should pain be the result"), CW, v. 72, pp. 387-88, 434, CW, v. 74, p. 368, CW, v. 89, p. 481.

27. CW, v. 68, p. 57. However, according to Gandhi, once having adopted the creed of nonviolence, one forswore the option of violent retaliation (CW, v. 74, pp. 64, 75, but cf. CW, v. 74, pp. 297-98, which seems to contradict this).

28. CW, v. 71, pp. 224-25.

29. CW, v. 68, pp. 137-38 ("canons"). Gandhi similarly defended Chinese armed resistance to Japanese aggression (CW, v. 68, p. 203).

30. CW, v. 68, pp. 137-38; cf. CW, v. 48, p. 106, "Zionism meaning reoccupation of Palestine has no attraction for me."

31. CW, v. 84, pp. 440-41.

32. See for example Simone Panter-Brick, *Gandhi and the Middle East: Jews, Arabs and imperial interests* (London: 2008).

33. CW, v. 87, p. 134 ("punishment"), CW, v. 89, pp. 242-43 ("traitors").

34. His occasionally nonjudgmental attitude also deserves notice. Thus he replied to a questioner:

    If like many others, nonviolence does not appeal to your heart, you should discard it. I shall not find fault with you for that, and, if others do, you should not care. The principle is this: "That which has been propounded by the *rishis* [poet-sages], practiced by the sages and appeals to one's heart should be followed and put into practice." The question might arise as to what one is to do when the thing that appeals to one's heart is contrary to what has been propounded by the *rishis* and practiced by the sages. The answer is, that in such a case the individual can follow his bent at his own risk. Many reforms and new discoveries have been made in this way. Our *Shankaracharyas* have supported the institution of untouchability but both our head and heart consider it a blot on Hinduism. We do not care if others consider our belief to be wrong. (CW, v. 85, p. 53; cf. CW, v. 46, p. 92)

35. CW, v. 66, p. 450.

36. CW, v. 42, p. 73 ("virtue"), CW, v. 74, pp. 75 ("impotent"), 83 ("unmanly"), CW, v. 79, p. 365 ("shortcoming"), HS, p. 44.

37. EW, p. 315. *Hind Swaraj* is rife with denunciations of "unmanly," "emasculated," and "effeminate" conduct, and praise for "manhood," "manliness" and "true men." It would be going too far afield to speculate on the roots of his cult of manliness. But briefly, Hindus (like Jews) suffered the stereotype of physical weakness while Muslims benefited from the stereotype of physical prowess (CW, v. 71, p. 72, EW, p. 199). It was therefore perhaps inevitable that a movement of national revival, even one pledged to nonviolence, would (like Zionism) put an accent on martial values. One might also note Gandhi's appropriation of military metaphors whereby he typically depicted himself as the "general" of an "army of

nonviolence" using "nonviolent arms" (for Gandhi's praise of aspects of the military regimen, cf. CW, v. 89, p. 332).

38. CW, v. 85, p. 281 ("impotence"), CW, v. 86, p. 132 ("police"); my emphases.

39. CW, v. 85, p. 235.

40. NR, pp. 132-33.

41. EW, p. 199.

42. CW, v. 61, pp. 265-66.

43. CW, v. 69, pp. 313-16. See also CW, v. 61, p. 316, CW, v. 66, pp. 420, 432, 439, CW, v. 67, pp. 11-12, 437, CW, v. 71, p. 235, CW, v. 74, pp. 92-93, 297-98, CW, v. 82, p. 302, CW, v. 85, pp. 11, 483, CW, v. 86, pp. 27, 80, 86, CW, v. 87, p. 201.

44. CW, v. 65, p. 361 ("reckless," "throwing"), CW, v. 74, p. 28, CW, v. 75, pp. 325-26.

45. CW, v. 66, p. 423, CW, v. 86, p. 89.

46. CW, v. 66, p. 436 ("fearless"), CW, v. 81, p. 438.

47. CW, v. 68, p. 191; but cf. CW, v. 69, pp. 291-92.

48. CW, v. 72, p. 224.

49. CW, v. 66, pp. 436, 449.

50. CW, v. 49, p. 91.

51. CW, v. 89, p. 225.

52. CW, v. 89, p. 129.

53. CW, v. 66, p. 398 ("strongest"), CW, v. 84, p. 12 ("wonderful"), EW, p. 348.

54. CW, v. 43, pp. 268-69 ("bullet"), CW, v. 66, pp. 407 ("emergency"), 447.

55. CW, v. 43, p. 93 ("befall"), CW, v. 66, p. 437 ("smilingly"), CW, v. 67, p. 437 ("cheerfully").

56. CW, v. 42, p. 397.

57. HS, p. 93.

58. CW, v. 67, p. 422.

59. HS, pp. 94-95.

60. CW, v. 43, p. 297.

61. CW, v. 43, pp. 327-28.

62. CW, v. 84, pp. 399-400; cf. CW, v. 43, p. 339, CW, v. 49, p. 496, CW, v. 51, p. 381, CW, v. 84, p. 423.

63. CW, v. 50, p. 171.

64. CW, v. 44, pp. 34 ("beneficial"), 164 ("friend"), 325 ("deliverance"), CW, v. 50, pp. 47 ("grand"), 296 ("boon"), CW, v. 87, p. 201.

65. CW, v. 44, pp. 212-13.
66. CW, v. 46, p. 252.
67. CW, v. 46, p. 343.
68. CW, v. 62, pp. 29-30 ("distrustful"), CW, v. 63, p. 59, CW, v. 66, p. 406.
69. NR, p. 154.
70. CW, v. 48, p. 431-35.

CHAPTER THREE

1. For Gandhi's own delineation of the various forms of *satya-graha*, see NR, pp. 214-15.
2. For the points in these paragraphs, see CW, v. 44, pp. 155-56, 184 ("deprivation"), CW, v. 51, pp. 73 ("ignorance"), 253, 316, CW, v. 53, pp. 228-30 ("Jesus"), 259 ("Jesus"), CW, v. 55, pp. 410-13, CW, v. 56, p. 369, CW, v. 72, p. 458, CW, v. 73, pp. 90-93, 156, CW, v. 80, p. 63, CW, v. 83, pp. 400-1 ("certain"), CW, v. 84, pp. 233-34 ("collections"), CW, v. 86, p. 105 ("duty"), NR, pp. 183, 193, 313-14, 331. For Gandhi's sexual experiments with young women, see CW, v. 86, pp. 414, 416, 420, 441-42, 452-53, 465-66, 475-76 ("noncooperation"), and Wolpert, *Gandhi's Passion*, pp. 225-30.
3. CW, v. 48, p. 243.
4. NR, p. 121.
5. CW, v. 74, pp. 164-65.
6. CW, v. 68, p. 30 ("roots"), EW, pp. 260-61, NR, pp. 131 ("intimidation"), 145. For a slightly bizarre scenario of Gandhi's, in which tenants cede to a voracious landlord more of their property than he actually demands or can use, thereby converting the landlord through cooperation (ceding the property), noncooperation (refusing to work any of the land) and love (giving him more than he requests), see CW, v. 72, pp. 226-27.
7. Gandhi also used the locution "passive resistance" to denote ersatz nonviolence ("nonviolence of the weak") and distinguish it from the genuine article.
8. NR, pp. 134-35 ("sufficient"), 155.
9. For Gandhi's sophistic defense of noncooperation as noncoercive, see NR, pp. 166-69, EW, p. 335.
10. Although exhorting picketers not to harass would-be patrons of a liquor store, Gandhi nonetheless granted: "But

one is permitted to cut off relationship with such individuals by way of [not] going to their homes for feasts on occasions such as marriages, and indeed one should do so. In short, they should not be harassed. The pain which they feel when we do not go to their homes for meals cannot be regarded as harassment" (CW, v. 46, p. 205). Yet, if not harassment, such ostracism still morally coerced: if the individuals stop imbibing alcohol, it might simply be to mitigate the pain of being shunned.

11. CW, v. 78, p. 224, NR, pp. 154 ("claimed"), 222, 229.

12. CW, v. 48, p. 338.

13. CW, v. 43, p. 126 ("touched"), CW, v. 46, p. 105 ("wildest"), CW, v. 51, pp. 167 ("sluggish"), 199 ("people"), CW, v. 55, p. 412 ("awaken"), CW, v. 68, p. 140 ("dignity"), CW, v. 69, p. 70 ("evoke"), CW, v. 78, p. 223 ("stir"), CW, v. 84, p. 372 ("eating"), CW, v. 86, p. 104 ("dead"), CW, v. 90, p. 202 ("sleeping"), NR, p. 35 ("sympathetic"). Gandhi is not altogether consistent on which faculty or organ *satyagraha* appeals to. Besides touching the conscience he speaks variously of wanting to "appeal . . . to the head and the heart," "appeal to the heart and soul of the people," and "touch the hearts" and make an "appeal to the highest in man," and "appealing to their reason and to their hearts." See CW, v. 43, p. 312, CW, v. 45, p. 222, CW, v. 48, p. 189, CW, v. 54, p. 417, CW, v. 55, p. 258, CW, v. 56, pp. 197-98, 254, CW, v. 58, p. 159, CW, v. 67, p. 195, CW, v. 78, p. 223, CW, v. 84, p. 372, NR, pp. 178, 181, 191, 202.

14. CW, v. 43, p. 392 ("result"), NR, pp. 77 ("mobilize"), 191.

15. CW, v. 68, p. 20.

16. EW, p. 249.

17. CW, v. 46, p. 313.

18. CW, v. 48, p. 483.

19. NR, p. 213.

20. CW, v. 44, p. 41, CW, v. 48, p. 405, CW, v. 53, p. 170 ("prejudice"), CW, v. 55, p. 1, CW, v. 79, p. 102, NR, pp. 6, 20, 193.

21. CW, v. 69, p. 212, CW, v. 84, p. 199 ("Nobody"), NR, p. 193. On a related point, Gandhi acknowledged that, even if mistaken, a sincerely held opinion cannot easily be dislodged (CW, v. 60, p. 500).

22. HS, p. 91 ("mistakes"), NR, p. 3.

23. EW, p. 357 (my emphasis).

24. In the case of such "personal" fasts, Gandhi set forth several preconditions for their success: (1) an affective bond must exist between the wrongdoer and the fasting penitent, otherwise the wrongdoer will experience the penitent's fast as "brute force" and "a form of coercion," not as born of love; (2) only a person having directly suffered on account of the wrongdoer can lay claim on a duty and right to do penance; (3) the penitent must not derive personal benefit from the wrongdoer's reformation, otherwise it becomes a species of extortion; (4) the wrongful act for which penance is being done must be morally unambiguous—"there should be no room for doubt as regards the fault . . . the wrong must be one that is accepted as such by society," otherwise it is "not penance but coercion" (CW, v. 50, pp. 193-97). Prima facie, and without saying more, it might be noticed that a fast by a loved one, and if only to correct a clear-cut moral failing, might still be experienced by the wrongdoer as coercive, and if the penitent suffered a direct loss on account of the wrongdoer's behavior, then the wrongdoer's reformation would be a direct gain for the penitent, and therefore a form of extortion.

CHAPTER FOUR

1. CW, v. 51, p. 118 ("rous[ing]," "duty"), CW, v. 53, p. 164 ("cultivating"), CW, v. 67, p. 350 ("force").

2. CW, v. 51, p. 62.

3. CW, v. 86, pp. 82 ("bona fides"), 126 ("friend").

4. The coinage was suggested to Gandhi by Untouchables, and he adopted it (CW, v. 82, p. 423, CW, v. 83, pp. 36, 365-66). In current usage, the Untouchables are properly referred to as Dalits.

5. CW, v. 51, pp. 126 ("stealthily"), 342 ("sting"), 344 ("ready"), 386, CW, v. 53, pp. 2, 7, 493 ("whole"). But when one of his early campaigns against untouchability turned brutal and bloody, Gandhi declared, "Loss even of a few hundred lives will not be too great a price to pay for the freedom of the 'unapproachables.' Only the martyrs must die clean" (NR, p. 187).

6. CW, v. 43, p. 137.

7. CW, v. 42, p. 373, CW, v. 48, pp. 9, 107, CW, v. 70, pp. 106 ("drink"), 224 ("ripe"), CW, v. 85, pp. 451-52 ("Smoking").

8. CW, v. 50, p. 289.

9. NR, pp. 189 ("break"), 190 ("hardest"), 197 ("stoniest").

10. CW, v. 43, p. 220 ("melt").

11. CW, v. 67, p. 284 ("opprobrium"). In the case of temple-entry Gandhi was at pains to stress that it was necessary to "accommodate the minority" opposed to such a reform because "mutual toleration is the law of the human family" (CW, v. 53, pp. 2-3, 6-8). He proposed granting Hindu fundamentalists limited hours or spaces of prayer in the temples with no Untouchables around.

12. CW, v. 80, p. 425.

13. CW, v. 73, pp. 279 ("dreadful"), 336 ("poorest"), CW, v. 87, p. 452 ("wiped out").

14. EW, p. 153 ("deliver"), CW, v. 78, p. 251 ("general").

15. CW, v. 43, p. 148 ("befitting"), CW, v. 44, p. 103 ("classified"), CW, v. 50, p. 213 ("appropriates"), CW, v. 72, p. 399 ("wherewithal"), CW, v. 85, pp. 114-15 ("exploitation"). For Gandhi's stringent standard of "non-stealing" (*asteya*), cf. CW, v. 44, pp. 90-91.

16. CW, v. 72, p. 381.

17. CW, v. 75, p. 158 ("gulf"), EW, p. 86 ("pauperism").

18. CW, v. 42, pp. 308-9, CW, v. 58, pp. 217-18 ("inherent"), CW, v. 61, p. 183 ("excess").

19. In fact, Gandhi conceived capitalism as a system of exploitation and, inasmuch as he opposed exploitation, his ultimate goal was proximate to that of the traditional Indian Left. Thus he counseled property-owners who "face the destruction wrought by strikers in their concerns":

> I would unhesitatingly advise such employers that they should at once offer the strikers full control of the concern which is as much the strikers' as theirs. They will vacate their premises not in a huff but because it is right, and, to show their goodwill, they would offer the employees the assistance of their engineers and other skilled staff. The employers will find in the end that they will lose nothing. Indeed, their right action will disarm opposition, and they will earn the blessings of their men. They will have made proper use of their capital. I

would not consider such action as benevolent. It would
be an intelligent use by the capitalists of their resources
and honest dealing in regard to the employees whom
they would have converted into honorable partners.
(CW, v. 83, p. 309)

See also CW, v. 42, pp. 275-76, CW, v. 58, pp. 29, 247, CW,
v. 67, p. 352, CW, v. 86, pp. 413, 423. Gandhi also embraced
the communist ideals of "to each according to his need" and
a "classless society," and described himself as a "socialist"
and a "communist" (CW, v. 45, pp. 298-99, CW, v. 83, pp.
26, 102, CW, v. 84, p. 5, CW, v. 85, pp. 7-8, CW, v. 88, pp. 261-
63, 282-83; but cf. CW, v. 88, pp. 14-18, 131-32, CW, v. 89, p.
406, for his occasionally harsh criticism of the tactics of the
party-affiliated Indian Left). On the other hand, he warned,
rightly, of the perils of nationalization by a "soulless" State
incarnating "violence in a concentrated and organized
form" (CW, v. 59, pp. 318-20; see also CW, v. 61, p. 183, CW,
v. 83, p. 27).

20. See CW, v. 78, p. 248, where a friendly critic of Gandhi al-
leges that the support he gets from a well-to-do Indian "pre-
vents radical reform," and CW, v. 84, p. 247, where Gandhi
defends himself, "Of course capitalists are among my friends
and I take pride in the fact that they accept me as a friend.
But I fight them when I feel there is need and no one fights
them harder. I fought the mill-owners as I suppose nobody
had fought them and successfully."

21. CW, v. 45, p. 299 ("awaken"), CW, v. 58, pp. 151-52 ("decency"), 218 ("kind," "ease"), 247 ("squander"), CW, v. 63, p.
404 ("blood-relations").

22. CW, v. 55, pp. 427-28.

23. See for example CW, v. 69, p. 219:

It may be asked as to how many trustees of this type one
can really find. As a matter of fact, such a question should
not arise at all. It is not directly related to our theory.
There may be just one such trustee or there may be none
at all. Why should we worry about it? We should have the
faith that we can, without violence or with so little violence that it can hardly be called violence, create such a
feeling among the rich. We should act in that faith.

See also CW, v. 45, p. 328, CW, v. 71, p. 28, CW, v. 72, p. 400.

24. CW, v. 45, pp. 339 ("Immediately"), 354 ("demonstrate"), CW, v. 48, p. 418 ("potent"), CW, v. 58, pp. 36 ("necessary"), 75-76 ("necessary"), 121-22 ("self-sacrificing"), CW, v. 59, p. 140, CW, v. 60, p. 254 ("educated"), CW, v. 67, p. 135, CW, v. 78, pp. 219-21 ("peasant"), CW, v. 82, p. 267 ("few").

25. CW, v. 72, p. 401.

26. CW, v. 42, p. 240.

27. Besides opposing class conflict because it entailed violence, Gandhi also believed that the capitalists possessed indispensable talents otherwise inaccessible to the working class (CW, v. 45, p. 339, CW, v. 63, p. 404, CW, v. 72, p. 400, CW, v. 87, p. 284). He somewhat demagogically dismissed class conflict as a "catchword" and "slogan" that was "imported from the West" and alien to "Eastern traditions" (CW, v. 58, pp. 219, 248); but cf. CW, v. 62, p. 46, where he qualifies, "The correspondent is wrong in suggesting that I do not believe in the existence of class struggle. What I do not believe in is the necessity of fomenting and keeping it up. I entertain a growing belief that it is perfectly possible to avoid it."

28. CW, v. 58, p. 29.

29. See CW, v. 42, p. 263, CW, v. 85, pp. 328-29, CW, v. 87, pp. 451-52, CW, v. 88, pp. 435-37, CW, v. 90, p. 495; but cf. CW, v. 42, p. 58, where he praises strikes as "a good weapon in the hands of workers for the removal of genuine grievances."

30. But see CW, v. 84, pp. 8-9, 102-3, 336, where Gandhi denounces a sweepers' strike because it used "coercion."

31. CW, v. 62, p. 29, CW, v. 67, p. 76 ("dignified," "retire"), CW, v. 68, p. 204 ("terrorism"), CW, v. 72, p. 188; but cf. CW, v. 68, pp. 137-41, where Gandhi purports that, if the Poles had disarmed, the "essential nature" of the invading Nazi and Soviet forces "would have made them desist from a wholesale slaughter of innocents."

32. CW, v. 68, p. 204, CW, v. 72, p. 383 ("defeat," "zest"), EW, p. 358.

33. CW, v. 62, p. 29, CW, v. 67, p. 415, CW, v. 72, p. 188 ("Imagine").

34. CW, v. 48, p. 421 ("corpses"), CW, v. 67, p. 405 ("soul"), CW, v. 68, pp. 204-5 ("annihilated," "glorious," "beginning").

35. CW, v. 72, p. 230, CW, v. 73, p. 322 ("Führer").

36. CW, v. 68, p. 205.

37. CW, v. 67, p. 405 ("novel"), CW, v. 68, pp. 189 ("fellow-feeling"), 191-92 ("bold"), 277 ("despair"), CW, v. 69, p. 122 ("species"), CW, v. 71, p. 407 ("Nero"), CW, v. 72, pp. 307 ("insane"), 361 ("duped"), CW, v. 73, p. 321 ("debased"), CW, v. 84, p. 420 ("patience"), CW, v. 86, pp. 156 ("monsters"), 302.

38. CW, v. 68, pp. 139 ("thanksgiving"), 405, CW. v. 69, p. 290 ("guillotine").

39. CW, v. 68, p. 138.

40. CW, v. 90, p. 522n2.

41. CW, v. 86, p. 100 ("done"), CW, v. 87, p. 200 ("Punjabis"), CW, v. 89, pp. 454-55 ("everybody").

42. CW, v. 68, p. 139.

43. Arthur Herman, *Gandhi and Churchill: The epic rivalry that destroyed an empire and forged our age* (New York: 2008); for Churchill's loathing of Gandhi and mockery of his nonviolent resistance, see pp. 509-11, 525; contrariwise, for Gandhi's respect for Churchill as a "great man," see CW, v. 89, p. 254.

44. CW, v. 42, pp. 487-88 ("benefits"), CW, v. 43, pp. 222-25 ("unmistakable"), CW, v. 86, p. 50 ("entrenched").

45. CW, v. 60, p. 50.

46. CW, v. 43, p. 7.

47. CW, v. 66, p. 104.

48. EW, p. 197.

49. CW, v. 84, p. 327.

50. CW, v. 48, pp. 168 ("fierce"), 352, 472, CW, v. 66, p. 104 ("notwithstanding"), CW, v. 73, p. 254 ("convert").

51. CW, v. 42, pp. 209 ("confirmed"), 484 ("destroy"), CW, v. 43, pp. 5-6 ("matching"), CW, v. 48, p. 231 ("obstacle"), EW, p. 197 ("force of will").

52. CW, v. 45, p. 311 ("conviction"), CW, v. 48, pp. 435 ("appreciate"; my emphasis), 454.

53. CW, v. 43, p. 6 ("deliberately"), CW, v. 45, pp. 366, 390, CW, v. 48, p. 185, NR, p. 74 ("public opinion"), HS, p. 115. See also CW, v. 82, p. 155, for Gandhi's distinction "between the Empire-builder Englishman of the old type . . . and the new type that is now coming into being, burning to make reparation for what his forefathers did"; but cf. CW, v. 45, p. 267, CW, v. 48, p. 435, CW, v. 79, p. 422, for Gandhi's verdict that "the British people have a faculty of self-delusion as no other

people have," and his skeptical opinion of "the average man in Europe or America."

54. CW, v. 43, pp. 179 ("world opinion"), 181, CW, v. 48, p. 397, CW, v. 51, pp. 132-33.

55. CW, v. 87, p. 75 ("quit"), CW, v. 88, p. 302 ("better").

CONCLUSION

1. Hugh Roberts, "Who Said Qaddafi Had to Go?," *London Review of Books* (17 November 2011).

www.ingramcontent.com/pod-product-compliance
Lightning Source LLC
Chambersburg PA
CBHW022104020426
42335CB00012B/817